Societal Complexity

The complexity of the modern world makes it difficult to predict the effects of political actions. In his 1997 book, *System Effects*, Robert Jervis underscored this difficulty by pointing to various sources of complexity when people interact. For example, they may misperceive each other's beliefs and motives, leading their actions to backfire or create unintended side effects. In this collection, scholars of international relations, law, network analysis, political philosophy, and political science examine why questions of societal complexity have become unfashionable in some social sciences and fashionable in others. And they discuss whether complex social interactions tie our hands: if our actions are unpredictable, should we, and can we, stop acting? Among the contributors are noted legal theorist Richard Posner; Philip E. Tetlock, the world's leading expert on the predictive shortcomings of experts; and Jervis himself, who contributes a retrospective look at his book and its lessons.

This book was originally published as a special issue of *Critical Review: A Journal of Politics and Society*.

Jeffrey Friedman is a visiting scholar in the Department of Government, University of Texas at Austin, USA. He received an MA in History from the University of California, Berkeley, USA, and a Ph.D. in Political Science from Yale University, USA. He is the founder and editor of *Critical Review: A Journal of Politics and Society*.

Societal Complexity
System Effects and the Problem of Prediction

Edited by
Jeffrey Friedman

LONDON AND NEW YORK

First published 2014
by Routledge

2 Park Square, Milton Park, Abingdon, Oxfordshire OX14 4RN
711 Third Avenue, New York, NY 10017

Routledge is an imprint of the Taylor & Francis Group, an informa business

First issued in paperback 2018

Copyright © 2014 Critical Review Foundation

All rights reserved. No part of this book may be reprinted or reproduced or utilised in any form or by any electronic, mechanical, or other means, now known or hereafter invented, including photocopying and recording, or in any information storage or retrieval system, without permission in writing from the publishers.

Notice:
Product or corporate names may be trademarks or registered trademarks, and are used only for identification and explanation without intent to infringe.

British Library Cataloguing in Publication Data
A catalogue record for this book is available from the British Library

ISBN13: 978-0-415-71296-5 (hbk)
ISBN13: 978-1-138-37744-8 (pbk)

Typeset in Garamond
by Taylor & Francis Books

Publisher's Note
The publisher accepts responsibility for any inconsistencies that may have arisen during the conversion of this book from journal articles to book chapters, namely the possible inclusion of journal terminology.

Disclaimer
Every effort has been made to contact copyright holders for their permission to reprint material in this book. The publishers would be grateful to hear from any copyright holder who is not here acknowledged and will undertake to rectify any errors or omissions in future editions of this book.

Contents

Citation Information   vii

1. Introduction: *System Effects* and the Problem of Prediction
   Jeffrey Friedman   1

2. The Complexity of System Effects
   Andrea Jones-Rooy and Scott E. Page   23

3. We Can Never Study Merely One Thing: Reflections on Systems Thinking and IR
   Nuno P. Monteiro   53

4. Jervis on Complexity Theory
   Richard A. Posner   77

5. Should "Systems Thinkers" Accept the Limits on Political Forecasting or Push the Limits?
   Philip E. Tetlock, Michael C. Horowitz, and Richard Herrmann   85

6. Conclusion: *System Effects* Revisited
   Robert Jervis   103

Index   127

Citation Information

The chapters in this book were originally published in *Critical Review: A Journal of Politics and Society*, volume 24, issue 3 (September 2012). When citing this material, please use the original page numbering for each article, as follows:

Chapter 1
Introduction: System Effects *and the Problem of Prediction*
Jeffrey Friedman
Critical Review: A Journal of Politics and Society, volume 24, issue 3 (September 2012)
pp. 291–312

Chapter 2
The Complexity of System Effects
Andrea Jones-Rooy and Scott E. Page
Critical Review: A Journal of Politics and Society, volume 24, issue 3 (September 2012)
pp. 313–342

Chapter 3
We Can Never Study Merely One Thing: Reflections on Systems Thinking and IR
Nuno P. Monteiro
Critical Review: A Journal of Politics and Society, volume 24, issue 3 (September 2012)
pp. 343–366

Chapter 4
Jervis on Complexity Theory
Richard A. Posner
Critical Review: A Journal of Politics and Society, volume 24, issue 3 (September 2012)
pp. 367–373

Chapter 5
Should "Systems Thinkers" Accept the Limits on Political Forecasting or Push the Limits?
Philip E. Tetlock, Michael C. Horowitz, and Richard Herrmann
Critical Review: A Journal of Politics and Society, volume 24, issue 3 (September 2012)
pp. 375–391

CITATION INFORMATION

Chapter 6
Conclusion: System Effects *Revisited*
Robert Jervis
Critical Review: A Journal of Politics and Society, volume 24, issue 3 (September 2012) pp. 393–415

Please direct any queries you may have about the citations to clsuk.permissions@cengage.com

Jeffrey Friedman

INTRODUCTION: *SYSTEM EFFECTS* AND THE PROBLEM OF PREDICTION

ABSTRACT: *Robert Jervis's* System Effects *(1997) shares a great deal with game theory, complex-systems theory, and systems theory in international relations, yet it transcends them all by taking account of the role of ideas in human behavior. The ideational element inserts unpredictability into Jervis's understanding of system effects. Each member of a "system" of interrelated actors interprets her situation to require certain actions based on the effects these will cause among other members of the system, but these other actors' responses to one's action will be based on their own perceptions of their situation and their interpretations of what it requires. These ideas are fallible, but we cannot predict the mistakes people will make if the errors are based on information we do not have or do not interpret in the same way they do. Not only members of a system but social-scientific observers and policy makers are ignorant of others' information and interpretations, and therefore are as likely to err in their behavioral predictions as are members of the system. Thus, Jervis's book raises serious questions about how to evaluate policies directed toward producing positive system effects. The questions are unanswerable at this point, but they might be susceptible to analysis by an ambitious form of political theory.*

Robert Jervis's *System Effects: Complexity in Political and Social Life* (Princeton University Press, 1997) is a classic work of political science that, unlike several that have previously been the subject of symposia here—Philip E. Converse's "The Nature of Belief Systems in Mass

---

Jeffrey Friedman, Critical Review Foundation, thanks Samuel DeCanio, Stephen DeCanio, and Nuno Monteiro for comments on previous drafts.

Publics" (1964), Jeffrey K. Tulis's *The Rhetorical Presidency* (1987), and Philip E. Tetlock's *Expert Political Judgment* (2005)[1]—did not come close to having the impact it should have had.

The problem may have been that the book was a poor fit with the subdisciplinary organization of political science. Jervis was a renowned scholar of international relations when he published this book; it was explicitly presented as an outgrowth of the structural neorealist international-relations theory of Kenneth Waltz (Jervis 1997, ch. 3); and most of Jervis's examples of system effects are historical incidents and developments in international affairs—that is, examples of the interaction of states, conceived as parts of an international system of states. However, as Nuno Monteiro (2012) points out below, international-systems theories do not satisfy the evidentiary criteria that international-relations scholars had begun to adopt when the book was published.

Moreover, while the book is unmistakably that of a scholar of international relations, it freely crosses sub-disciplinary (and disciplinary) boundaries, drawing from public policy, American politics, and domestic politics to develop the key themes of systemic nonlinearities, feedback effects, indirect effects, and the effects of contingency, all of which are building blocks of complex-systems theory. It is only natural, then, to read the book as an application to politics of complex-systems theory (as opposed to international-systems theory), as Andrea Jones-Rooy and Scott E. Page (2012) do below.[2]

Jervis as Complex-Systems Theorist

However, Jervis builds something rather unusual from the standard elements of complex-systems theory. For example, he writes that in politics, "differences in expectations and policy preferences are often rooted in different beliefs about feedbacks" (Jervis 1997, 130), and he spends much of his chapter 4 discussing how, in turn, these different beliefs affect political behavior through their influence on preferences and expectations. And among the phenomena caught in Jervis's net are interaction effects, which are not so readily fit into the complex-systems framework, since, as Jervis defines them, they change "the environment of action, so that other actors do not respond as anticipated" (Jervis 2012, 395). When anticipations are frustrated, as when expectations and preferences are formed (as opposed to being posited by the theorist), we cannot be discussing the interactions of thoughtless biological organisms or mindlessly rule-following automata (Mitchell 2009), which are the actors in classic systems-theory computer modeling (Page 2011, 42–43). "System effects can occur with inanimate objects," Jervis (1997, 253) observes, "but greater complexities are introduced with human beings whose behavior is influenced by their expectations of what others will do, who realize that others are influenced by their expectations of the actor's likely behavior, and who have their own ideas about system effects."

This passage, and the many strategic interactions discussed by Jervis, convey the game-theoretic dimension of the book, in which systemically connected adversaries try to outguess each other. Game theory has as much affinity as complex-systems theory with Jervis's project. Yet game theory still misses a crucial element, because it requires the modeler to predict the players' reactions to each other's actions. Jervis, however, contends that "to claim that we can be certain of how each actor will respond, how the different behaviors will interact, and how people will then adjust to the changed circumstances goes beyond the knowledge we can have" (Jervis 1997, 72).

The key to understanding this contention is, I think, found in Jervis's previously quoted claim that human beings introduce extra complexities because they "have their own ideas about system effects." Arguably, this is because people have access to different information about whatever systems they are entangled in, and because they interpret this information differently. "Few social acts fail to alter the informational as well as the physical environment," Jervis (1997, 145) writes, and no given datum is known to all or understood in the same terms by all. Thus, "disagreements [about the likely consequences of an action] are not surprising" (ibid., 73), and the divergent information streams and interpretive responses that lead different agents to disagree about the consequences of their actions—i.e., to disagree about their actions' likely system effects—cannot be transcended by those who are trying to predict the agents' behavior. The observers at Time 1, like the agents themselves, are trying to discern the best action for the agents to take, and in both cases this depends on forecasts of various possible actions' results—in the form of other actors' reactions—at Time 2. But since neither actors nor observers can know in advance how other actors in the system will perceive, interpret, and (after again forecasting the results of various actions) respond to T_1 actions, the reliability of actors'/observers' forecasts about behavior at T_2 is questionable at best.

Jervis as Political Scientist

Accordingly, the book is notably retrospective, as Richard A. Posner (2012) emphasizes below. Jervis issues no predictions and constructs no formal models.[3] He does adduce plentiful examples of various patterns of interactive behavior and mistake, but he is not constructing a political "science" in the sense that he assumes that he is describing universal behavioral laws.

In perhaps the most formalistic and "law-like" passage in the book (one that is of no great importance to the overall argument), Jervis (1997, 216) writes that states are

> likely to develop good relations with each other if they share allies. It will be difficult for both A and C to maintain their close ties with B if they are adversaries. If the alliance with B is highly valued, A and C will have to mute their quarrels, and the desire to increase the coalition's strength will give both A and C incentives to bring the other into the fold. There will be a cost, however, if the main target of the alliance between A and B is not the same as that between C and B. In this case, if A and C join together they will not only bolster each other, which they will resist doing if they have bilateral conflicts, but also will pay the price of taking on the other's adversaries. For these reasons, the impact of having a common friend is less than that of having a common adversary; systems are more likely to be unbalanced by not having those with common allies be themselves allies than they are by having states fail to unite in the face of a common adversary.

However, even when Jervis draws generalizations like this one, they are expressed as mere "likelihoods," and they are clearly conditioned upon motives and knowledge that may not be present in a given case, and that may be counteracted by other factors if they are present. In short, they are Weberian ideal types: logically coherent explanations of what will happen *if* (1) certain presuppositions hold, and (2) other factors do not intervene.

While it is typical for social scientists to attach *ceteris paribus* clauses to their predictions, meeting Weber's second criterion, Jervis takes the clause seriously enough to notice that it rarely holds good, rendering prediction unreliable. Perhaps more importantly, where most social scientists ignore the first criterion, Jervis does not. That is, he does not assume that the preconditions of an ideal type will be applicable to all cases *as long as* the *ceteris paribus* clause holds good.

The assumption of uniformity in underlying causes allows incautious social scientists to infer future behavior from past behavior (as long as the *ceteris paribus* clause holds good). But Weber ([1904] 1949) viewed the purpose of social science as purely historical, and the purpose of historical research as the discovery of *whether* an ideal type's preconditions are applicable to a given case. If, by contrast, ideal types expressed lawlike regularities, then historical research could only be directed toward seeing if, in a given case, the underlying tendency was overridden by some other factor (violating the *ceteris paribus* clause). Weber's own historical research culminated in a bold, bleak understanding of modernity as the hyper-rationalized product of contingent chains of events in intellectual and cultural history (especially the history of religion). Since there was no underlying necessity to these events, they could not be used as the basis for predictions of the future. But in that case, what was the point of social science, i.e., historical research? To clarify the nature and roots of our present condition.

A more typical Jervisian statement immediately follows the passage I have extracted above:

> States can also manipulate the dynamics that produce consistency in order to produce a desired alignment: If a state wants to make or solidify an alliance with another, it may pick a quarrel with the other's adversary. In the previous chapter, I noted A. J. P. Taylor's argument that in order to draw France into his orbit, Bismarck created a colonial conflict with France's adversary, Great Britain. Greater evidence supports the view that one reason why Anwar Sadat distanced himself from the USSR in late 1972 was his belief that this would bring financial assistance from the conservative and anticommunist Arab oil kingdoms. While Nixon and Kissinger did not create the crisis between India and Pakistan in 1971, they did realize that the resulting friction between the U.S. and India would increase the common interest between the U.S. and China. The same reasoning explains why British leaders foresaw some gain in the Ottoman Empire's siding with Germany in 1914: "The best method of persuading the Balkan States to join the Allies would be alliance against their common and traditional enemy, the Turk." (Jervis 1997, 216)

What is being expressed in these examples are fruitions of an underlying *possibility*, not the operation of an underlying law. The aim of Jervis's retrospective focus, however, is not entirely Weberian. Although Jervis does use ideal types to explain the past, he also goes a step further by pointing out the applicability of given ideal types to *many* actual historical situations. He is looking for regularities, not trying to explain (except incidentally) how we got to where we are.

Still, in his treatment of the regularities he finds, he does not take the fatal additional step of claiming that they are products of knowable universal laws that would enable the prediction of future cases (except inasmuch as we can always predict that *if* the presuppositions of an ideal type *do* apply in a future case and are not counteracted, *then* we can expect certain results).

It is true that by backing away from the enunciation of universal laws, Jervis remains in line with most political scientists' *explicit* agendas; only a minority of empirical political scientists claim that their findings can be duplicated everywhere and always, such that they can be used to predict the future.[4] International relations is the most predictively oriented subfield of political science (Monteiro and Ruby 2009); here Jervis's book makes a striking contrast. Yet even in the other empirical subfields, the positivist notion that everything must ultimately be reducible to (knowable) universal laws displays its hold in excrescences such as quadrennial attempts to derive formulae for predicting the next presidential election outcome, usually on the basis of "real" (economic) factors.[5] Even if one follows Milton Friedman (1953) in insisting that the factors expressed by such formulae are not supposed to be *actually* causing electoral outcomes, but are merely variables that (for some unknown reason) allow us to make good behavioral predictions, in practice one usually wants to know what *is* actually causing the behavior, and it is all too easy to assume that whatever is causing it—since it seems to be responsible for a behavioral regularity—must be some universal human disposition.

Indeed, one would only think to test factors such as economic growth as predictors of voting behavior because one finds it plausible that voters are, at bottom—past, present, and future—members of the species *Homo economicus*. However, when one moves from treating objective economic variables as mere predictive instruments to treating them as "real" causal factors, one is tacitly assuming that voters are somehow able to *know* the economic variables; if they did not, for example, know that there was a recession, they could not respond to it by voting against the incumbent.[6] (This applies even to retrospective-voting models that are intended to minimize voters' need for information.)[7] But aggregate economic factors are not self-evident to anyone; they must be mediated. How would even an unemployed voter know whether the business she used to work for had closed because of a recession or, alternatively, because of management errors or some combination of factors? The very concept of a recession—like the questions of whether a recession is occurring and why—must somehow be theorized and communicated to voters; one cannot directly observe a recession, let alone identify its sources, but instead must hypothesize that certain accessible facts (such as one's own unemployment, or an unemployment figure heard on the news) are politically relevant because of government actions or inaction that caused or allowed the "recession." The causal force behind regularities such as those identified by election forecasters must therefore be voters' subjective ideas, however inchoate, about objective economic conditions and their causes—not the conditions and causes themselves.

To the extent that subjective ideas are mistaken, models based on "real" factors will produce equally mistaken forecasts—i.e., they will be unrealistic.[8] Thomas Holbrook and James C. Garand (1996) suggest that most voters in the 1992 election severely overestimated the straits the economy was in. Marc J. Hetherington (1996) shows that during the 1992 campaign, the media failed adequately to report that the recession that had occurred under the incumbent had ended twenty months before the election, and that voters who were most heavily exposed to the media had the most inaccurate impressions about economic performance. So the incumbent lost, and the opposition candidate's slogan was "It's the Economy, Stupid." Such empirical anomalies (from the perspective of those who view objective factors as determinative) get washed out by the aggregates used by the forecasters.[9]

The assumption that any regularity must reflect universal tendencies may also lead to *illogical* answers to the question of what those tendencies really represent. An example is the fact that rational-ignorance theory is often casually thought to explain twentieth-century U.S. voters' political ignorance. According to this theory, the regularly observed fact that most twentieth-century American voters show little awareness of political events, personages, and policy debates can be explained by the fact that voters realize that any one vote is unlikely to affect the outcome of an election with many voters, so they rationally calculate that it would be a waste of time for them to pay attention to political news. However, if they *knew* that their votes were unlikely to affect the outcome, and if their motive in voting were to affect the outcome, then they would abstain from voting rather than deliberately underinform themselves before voting.[10]

The massive reality of voting thus precludes the applicability of rational-ignorance theory to anyone but *nonvoters*. Yet the theory persists. It is hard to avoid the conclusion that it persists because of an unexamined slide from the identification of patterns of political ignorance in recent American political history to the conclusion that since all political behavior is lawlike, any regularity implies a knowable, universal cause.[11] Such a cause must, by definition, be an objective fact—whether the unemployment rate or the odds against one's vote mattering in a large electorate. Yet objective facts can influence one's conscious decisions only if one subjectively perceives them and interprets them as germane to one's decision.

Thus, all positivism will in one way or another have to minimize the importance of subjective beliefs. The usual means to this end is to assume tacitly that the ideas of the agents whose behavior one is trying to predict (or retrodict) are identical to one's own.[12] Thus, electoral predictions based on economic statistics, and explanations of voter ignorance by means of rational choice, both minimize subjectivity by assuming, in effect, that voters know the facts the theorist takes to be crucial (economic variables or the odds that a vote will matter); and by further assuming that the voters know, and agree with, the theories that make the political scientists think that those facts "should" in some sense decide the agents' actions. Yet positivists routinely fail to identify mechanisms by which these facts and interpretations might plausibly be *communicated* to the agents whose actions are being predicted—and communicated in precisely the same form that has made them persuasive to the positivist scholar. Technically speaking, positivism—by which I simply mean predictive social science—substitutes ontology (objective facts) for epistemology (some mechanism by which agents can perceive objective facts and interpret their significance for agents' future actions).

Jervis as Political Epistemologist

In *Perceptions and Misperceptions in International Politics* (1976), Jervis pointed out that in the study of international relations, too, scholars routinely "explain and predict" actions by inferring the appropriate behavior of an agent confronting given objective environmental factors (ibid., 16). In response, Jervis observed that foreign-policy decision makers could themselves could use the same method of inference: If they

> believed that the [objective] setting is crucial they would not need to scrutinize the details of [another] state's recent behavior or try to understand the goals and beliefs held by the state's decision-makers. It would be fruitless and pointless to ask what the state's intentions are if its behavior is determined by the situation in which it finds itself. Instead, observers would try to predict how the context will change because this will tell them what the state's response will be. Decision-makers could then freely employ their powers of vicarious identification and simply ask themselves how they would act if they were in the other's shoes. They would not have to worry about the possibility that the other might have values and beliefs that differed from theirs. It is interesting, although not decisive, to note that decision-makers rarely feel confident about using this method. They usually believe both that others may not believe as they would and that the decision-makers within the other state differ among themselves. So they generally seek a great deal of information about the views of each significant person in the other country. (Ibid.)

Presumably Jervis allows that this type of information seeking by decision makers does not decisively refute the notion that behavior can be predicted from objective circumstances because the decision makers could be wrong: Contrary to their belief that subjective perceptions cannot be read unambiguously from objective circumstances, it could be that these circumstances are so obvious to all that "decision-makers usually perceive the world quite accurately" (Jervis 1976, 3), as the social scientists assume. However, if the decision makers of country A are trying to infer country B's decision makers' subjective perceptions of objective conditions, it can only be because the decision makers in country A think that the perceptions of those in country B may differ from objective reality (as interpreted by those in country A). From the social scientists' perspective, this constitutes a serious mistake by the actors in country A whose behavior they are trying to predict. It is a mistake not only about the importance of the subjective perceptions of country B's decision makers, but (therefore) about the *objective* environment A's decision makers face, which consists, in large part, of the behavior and potential behavior of other states' decision makers. It will not do, then, to predict the behavior of A from the objective environment, since A's decision makers evidently fail to understand that environment—falsifying the assumption that the environment is unambiguous to all.

Because *System Effects* is almost entirely retrospective, Jervis is able to avoid the logical fallacies and empirical overgeneralizations that so many of his colleagues commit. But one might also say that the book *had* to be retrospective because of the crucial element that Jervis adds to game theory and complex-systems theory: attention to the unpredictable subjective beliefs about objective reality that are prerequisites for political action. To the extent that beliefs govern behavior, and to the extent that they are unpredictable, then clearly we cannot predict future behavior. We may be able to infer past beliefs from past behavior by applying an ideal typology to the behavior. But we will be unable to predict the applicability to a future situation of an ideal type that is contingent on actors' beliefs. Thus, reliable forecasts of human behavior would appear to be out of bounds.

Why, however, should we think that subjective beliefs are unpredictable? Building on Jervis's 1976 argument, one might first of all note that reasonable people could not *disagree* about the best course of action in a given circumstance if that course of action could be unambiguously derived from the facts alone. We have already seen that Jervis has shown that foreign-policy decision makers disagree with international-relations scholars who claim that their adversaries' actions can be unambiguously derived from the facts alone. If scholars and policy makers can disagree, cannot policy makers themselves disagree?

Much of *System Effects* is devoted to exemplifying just such disagreement. For instance, Jervis (1997, 45) notes that "many cases of intelligence failure are mutual—i.e., they are failures by the side that took the initiative as well as by the state that was taken by surprise." We can stop right there: A state could hardly be surprised by another state's actions if the decision makers and intelligence analysts of the two states agreed with each other on the objective facts and on how to interpret them. Yet "the U.S. did not expect the Russians to put missiles into Cuba or Japan to attack Pearl Harbor because American officials knew that the U.S. would thwart these measures if they were taken. These judgments were correct, but because the other countries saw the world and the U.S. less accurately, the American predictions were also inaccurate" (ibid.).

Decision makers may also disagree among themselves, not just with their counterparts in other states. For example,

> [an] agent's beliefs about what tactics are appropriate may ... differ from the views of those at home. The man on the spot almost always feels he knows more about the local situation than his superior and believes many of his instructions to be hopelessly out of touch with the reality he sees. His superiors, he is apt to conclude, do not understand what is happening or what can be achieved. ...
>
> An agent's disobedience can take various forms. In some cases an agent may refuse to deliver a message or may substitute one of his own for that of his government. In negotiations with Portugal in 1943 George Kennan gave the Portuguese government an assurance that was "in direct violation of the written orders I had in my safe." ... In 1809 the British minister to the United States broke his instructions and signed a treaty with America that did not meet major British demands. (Jervis 1976, 332–33)

Jervis also adduces a case that might have had a significant effect on Hitler's expansionism: the British ambassador to Germany appended to his official protest against the *Anschluss* the caveat that Austria "'had acted with precipitate folly.'" This may not only have encouraged Hitler, if he misunderstood it as a signal of the British government's real attitude; it may have discouraged the British government from taking further measures to express its resolve against Nazi expansionism, since the ambassador did not report his remarks to his superiors (ibid., 333–34).

Given that one's best course of action in a system will depend on its consequences once other actors perceive one's action and respond to it (if they do); and assuming, for the sake of argument, shared values among the decision makers;[13] then all decision makers would derive the best course of action from objective circumstances if this could be done unambiguously. In that case, there would be no disagreement among decision makers. Thus, unless one minimizes the possibility that the actual disagreement that we routinely encounter is *reasonable*—e.g., by ascribing disagreement to irrational emotions, which could perhaps be forecast (with the assistance of psychology)—the project of predicting human behavior faces a serious obstacle in what might be called "the fact of genuine disagreement." Genuine disagreement among reasonable decision makers who are aiming at the same end is as anomalous for those who would predict human behavior as voting is for those who would attribute voters' political ignorance to their knowledge that their individual vote does not matter.

Disagreement about the best course of action also indicates that one or both of the parties to the disagreement is in error, as is clearly evident in

Jervis's take on Soviet and American predictions of each other's actions before the Cuban Missile Crisis and Japanese and American predictions of each other's actions before Pearl Harbor. If we could predict people's beliefs and thus their actions from their objective circumstances, such errors would be impossible. A world of predictable human beings would be a world of infallible human beings. Our predictions will be frustrated to the extent that mistakes are made by those whose actions we would presume to predict—unless we share in the same mistaken logic or faulty information stream that might have led those particular actors to err. But if the content of the information to which one is exposed varies from person to person or changes over time, we cannot possibly share in the information streams that will be available to those whose actions we try to predict. To the extent that their subjective perceptions are based on those streams, we will not be able to predict their perceptions, hence their actions.

Finally there is a fact that receives great emphasis in *System Effects*. Those whose behavior we might want to predict are not just trying to outguess each other's strategic moves; they are, more generally, trying to forecast what will happen when their actions, and others' actions, react against, and contribute to, the objective realities that everyone in a system is trying to perceive and predict. In short, the objective realities themselves change as actors interpret them and take actions based on their interpretations. A belief-dependent objective reality can no more be forecast than can the beliefs themselves.

This raises the question of what human "systems" really are. They can be loosely defined as webs of interacting agents, but the agents' interactions derive from perceptions of reality, not from some other (ontological) dimension of reality. If a "state" exists deep in the Amazon, unknown to the outside world, it is ontologically real but it is not part of "the state system." If a state that is part of that system (because it is perceived as such) builds a nuclear reactor for military purposes but portrays it as a peaceful source of electric power, there is an "interaction" only if analysts in other states see through the ruse, or suspect that it might be a ruse. Yet their suspicions may be unfounded—the perception of a threat may be mistaken—in which case the interaction is grounded not in ontology but in an erroneous theory held by the decision makers who misperceive the reactor as a threat. This does not, of course, make the interaction itself unreal. On the contrary: perceptions are real, and they can lead to real actions.

If one were to diagram these interactions, as Jones-Rooy and Page diagram various networks, all the action would be in the arrows between agents, but these would express *the observer's* theories about the theories agents have, or should have, about each other's theories (as well as "real" factors such as their military capabilities), and therefore about each other's likely actions. While subjective perceptions are objective realities in themselves, and while the objects of these perceptions may have "real" correlates, including actions, the system of interactions is an expression only of epistemological relationships, not extra-ideational realities.[14]

The "complexity" of the human environment to which Jervis refers may therefore best be seen as a product of the limits on our ability to understand and especially predict it, not as a product of its inherent qualities, such as nonlinearities, feedback effects, indirect effects, and the effects of contingency.[15] This is to suggest further that what makes a human system complex is not its nonlinear emergence as such, nor its "spontaneity," nor the number of factors that interact within it.[16] It is the difficulty of understanding and predicting the ideas of other people—those with whom we directly and indirectly interact, and those whom we, as scholars, observe or imagine directly and indirectly interacting.

Jervis as Political Theorist

System effects, in this view, are caused by the fallible perceptions of people who are each trying to formulate accurate predictions of others' behavior based on their interpretations of what seems to them relevant evidence about each other's beliefs. Disagreements among agents who are pursuing the same goal indicate error on the part of some or all of them (although, given the limits of human knowledge, consensus would not necessarily indicate the absence of error). In turn, the fact that Jervis builds human error into his understanding of society puts him at odds with those who would predict human behavior: not just social scientists, but policy makers; and not just foreign-policy makers, but domestic-policy makers—be they voters, elected officials, appointed officials, or bureaucrats. They, too, are (sometimes unwittingly) predicting the effect of proposed actions on a human system (a polity). Thus, while Jervis's brand of political epistemology makes an uneasy fit with international-relations theory, complex-systems theory, and game theory, it may yet provide instruction to normative political theorists.

Jervis (1997, 60) summarizes the upshot of fallible policy predictions (and of simplistic attempts to understand the roots of policy failures after the fact) by saying that "intentions and outcomes often are very different, regulation is prone to misfire, and our standard methodologies are not likely to capture the dynamics at work." Indeed, *System Effects* opens with an epigraph from a *New Yorker* story about marine biologist Sylvia A. Earle, in which Jervis (ibid., 3) ironically juxtaposes Earle's conviction that one needs to be aware of "the continuing interconnectedness of the system" (White 1989, 56) against her declaration that, to minimize oil spills, we should "mandate double-hulled vessels and compartments in tankers" (ibid., 46). Jervis points out that

> it seems obvious that if tankers had double hulls, there would be fewer oil spills. But interconnections mean that the obvious and immediate effect might not be the dominant one. The straightforward argument compares two worlds, one with single-hulled tankers and one with double-hulled ones, holding everything else constant. But in a system, *everything else will not remain constant*. The shipping companies, forced to purchase more expensive tankers, might cut expenditures on other safety measures, in part because of the greater protection supplied by the double hulls. The relative cost of alternative means of transporting oil would decrease, perhaps moving spills from the seas to the areas traversed by the new pipelines. But even tanker spills might not decrease. The current trade-off between costs and spills may reflect the preferences of shippers and captains, who might take advantage of the greater safety by going faster and taking more chances. If double hulls led to even a slight increase in the price of oil, many other consequences could follow, from greater conservation, to increased uses of alternative fuels, to hardship for the poor. (Ibid., 8)

Notice that the barrier to accurate prediction here is purely epistemological. If we could—in advance—read the minds of the agents about whom Jervis is speculating, there would be no problem in deciding whether to mandate double hulls.

Jervis is using standard microeconomic analysis of cost-benefit decision making—yet the analysis is couched as speculation. An economist could assert that, *ceteris paribus*, the things that Jervis says *might* happen *will* happen. But even setting aside the propriety of thus assuming that one knows the uniform underlying causes of human behavior in given situations, the *ceteris paribus* clause renders such assertions useless as policy advice. Take the more familiar case of the minimum wage. The mere claim that, *ceteris paribus*, an increase of $X per hour in the legal minimum *must* cause more unemployment is wrong: If the increase is $.01, it may cause no unemployment at all. Nor can we know the level at which this will no longer be the case. So a *ceteris paribus* clause will, for policy purposes, at least have to be translated into a "tendency" for the wage increase to cause unemployment. Yet if the tendency may amount to zero this prediction is useless, and if the tendency translates into one or a hundred or a thousand people unemployed, policy makers may think that this cost is outweighed by the benefit of higher wages for the remaining low-wage workers.

A policy prediction must therefore have a quantity attached to it if it is to be of any service. Here economists oblige by conducting empirical research, but, of necessity, economists' studies focus on past times and places, often producing widely varying results—not surprisingly, if we do not assume that people everywhere and always will have the same *ideas* about how to respond to a regulation such as a minimum-wage increase (or a double-hull requirement).[17] Economists often proceed as if the variations in their empirical results can be ignored in favor of concluding that the "weight of the evidence" reveals that, say, minimum wages tend (or do not tend) to increase unemployment, but again, this presumes what is at issue—whether *knowable* (indeed, in this case, *known*) underlying laws are at work—and it does not produce a quantitative estimate.[18] To produce such an estimate, the economist as "policy scientist" must combine the results of past research into formulae that, like election predictions, will yield precise numbers—but only by, again, begging the epistemological question. The question is whether observers can reliably predict the behavioral reactions that policy actions will cause. Even if these reactions were based on the same unambiguous objective conditions that might explain data from the past, there would remain the problem of predicting what these conditions will be in the future. But if the people who react to the policy had and will have varied perceptions of the new situation caused by the policy, and divergent theories about how to respond to it, then unless we can read their minds, our point predictions will not be likely to hit their mark.

In short, an economic policy "science" is precisely as scientific as clairvoyant telepathy is. This is true of any other would-be policy science, too, where changes in human behavior are the aim of the policy. Does this lead to the conclusion that we should not make public policy?

The question is nonsensical, as "inaction" cannot be logically distinguished from "action." The only choice is between various predictions of system effects: Will a particular *new* "state" action produce better results than would the mere continuation of the whole ensemble of previously enacted regulations (e.g., legal enforcement of a certain bundle of private-property rights), or would refraining from the new action produce better results? Given the hazards of prediction discussed by Jervis, it is tempting to throw up our hands and say that we cannot possibly know. This is the dilemma discussed by Posner (2012) and by Philip E. Tetlock, Michael C. Horowitz, and Richard Herrmann (2012) below.

Jervis's solution, in his contribution to the symposium (Jervis 2012), is more pessimistic than it was in *System Effects*, which ended with a catalogue of general recommendations for making public policy more robust against system effects. Jervis concluded that the possibility of these effects does not entail

> that reforms must fail or that directed change is impossible, but that the game does not end after one or two plays and that new measures will be needed to cope with the new problems. So in criticizing the quotation with which I began this book, I do not mean to imply that it is a mistake to require tankers to have double hulls, but only that doing so would have multiple consequences, some of which could defeat the purpose unless other actions are taken. They can be, however: Special instructions and training could be given to ships' captains, additional taxes might be levied on pipelines, and officials could be ready to respond to the undesired consequences of these supplementary policies. (Jervis 1997, 294)

Now, however, he writes that "although I closed my book with a discussion of how understanding system effects can lead actors to take advantage of them, I would not want to claim that this is always possible. We should always ask of an action, 'What will follow, and how will we and others react and change?' But we should also realize the limits to our ability to answer, or at least to do so correctly" (Jervis 2012, 412).

Perhaps Jervis came to realize that fixes such as those he had suggested as add-ons to the double-hull mandate cannot be known in advance to work, any more than we can know whether the fixes would respond to actual problems caused by the mandate: Jervis was, after all, at least as I interpret him, not providing us with ironclad predictions of the negative unintended consequences such a regulation would produce, but instead with a list of *possible* unintended consequences. To be more schematic, these possibilities, drawn from the application of neoclassical economic theory to the policy advocated by Earle, are known (to Jervis) as unknowns. (To Earle, they seem to have been unknown unknowns.)[19] Yet even if we know of ten possible negative unintended consequences of a given policy, we cannot know which of these effects will justify a policy response unless we can predict whether they are not mere logical possibilities but "tendencies" and, if so, what their magnitude is likely to be.

If economics provided the best account of unintended consequences, we would have to leave the matter there and simply recommend that policy makers be as sensitive as possible to the known unknowns identifiable by thinking about the incentives new policies might create. However, Jervis's books provide the basis for a better account: a theory of unintended consequences grounded in epistemic failure, not misaligned incentives. Although Jervis often invokes the incentive of actors to circumvent new regulations (Jervis 1997, ch. 2), his analysis does not *rely* on incentives: "The results of actions are often unintended and . . . regulations often misfire," he writes, because "actors can rarely be fully constrained and will react in ways that those who seek to influence them are unlikely to foresee or desire" (ibid., 91). As we have seen in the cases drawn from foreign policy, this unpredictability need not depend on the incentive to outwit an opponent; Japanese and U.S. decision makers had every incentive not to misperceive each other's intentions, yet they did. Their acts of misinterpretation were unintended consequences of each other's previous actions and led to further, disastrous unintended consequences. The bad news is that this makes the task of prediction even harder than it is when we are trying to select the likeliest from a group of known unknowns generated by economic theory. How can we possibly predict the likelihood of unknown unknowns?

If the general source of unintended consequences is epistemological, not motivational, it is hard to imagine how we could try to predict them case by case (policy by policy), but we might be able to get some traction if we move to a more general level, asking fundamental questions such as whether unknown unknowns might, overall, be positive rather than negative: surely no law dictates that mistaken beliefs cannot lead to serendipitous results. Then there is the question of degree. For expository purposes I have presupposed a binary distinction between the predictability and the unpredictability of ideas, hence the unpredictability of behavior; this is clearly an exaggeration. We are not completely opaque to each other, and in consequence, evidence of each other's thinking is not uniformly ambiguous. If we could pin down the sources of our occasional interpersonal transparency, we might be able to make suggestions about institutions that might capitalize on them. We might also be able to discern which types of problem-solving are likely to be vulnerable to negative rather than positive unintended consequences. Tetlock is engaged in a sweeping long-term study of effective prediction strategies, based on his disturbing findings about the errors made by experts trying to predict relatively simple future events (Tetlock 2005). The approach I am suggesting would be even more intellectually ambitious, since the causes of interpersonal opacity (and transparency) may be related to such factors as biological and cultural evolution; and the institutional upshots of such factors would have to take into account, on the one hand, the differences between contemporary human relationships and institutions and their biological and cultural predecessors and, on the other hand, the potential directions in which fallible, ideational beings might be advised to go.

Jervis's contribution, then, may not fit into disciplinary pigeonholes because it points to a type of grand political theorizing—theorizing about the human condition—that would be appropriate only to normative political theory. And even in that subfield, such theorizing has long been out of style.

NOTES

1. On Converse, see *Critical Review* 18, nos. 1–3 (2006), republished as Friedman and Friedman 2012a; on Tulis, *Critical Review* 19, nos. 2–3 (2007), republished as Friedman and Friedman 2012b; on Tetlock, *Critical Review* 22, no. 4 (2010).
2. Mitchell 2009 is an excellent guidebook to complex-systems theory, not least in that the author frequently asks whether the theory is applicable to human realities, and does not hesitate to answer in the negative.
3. Sometimes, to be sure, he imports law-like generalizations from other disciplines, such as psychology, writing, for example, that "people tend to think that good things (and bad things) go together and thereby minimize the perceived trade-offs among desired values" (Jervis 1997, 230) and then citing a slew of psychology-journal articles. (Jervis 1976 is an extended engagement with the cognitive-psychology literature aimed at producing generalizations about the basis of misperceptions.) However, if there is one field that, in principle, *might* impose regularities on what would otherwise be the kaleidoscopic flux of

ideational possibilities, it would be psychology, since the members of a species might well share cognitive traits that constrain their ideas. This is not to say, however, that the reading I am giving would be endorsed by Jervis. I am trying to ferret out the logical prerequisites and implications of system effects as he presents them, but sometimes readers of the book will find statements, particularly in chapter 1, that run counter to my interpretation of this logic, particularly on pages 22 and 144, where Jervis casually refers to the "laws" of economics and, on page 22, of politics. (However, Jervis does not identify these laws or claim to be adding to them.) I construe this as a case of his not having fully appreciated the radically antipositivist implications of the book.

4. It does not take a leap of the imagination, however, to "predict" that political scientists might jump on the Nate Silver bandwagon and use statistics to try to predict things other than elections. See Ward and Metternich 2012. For a pre-emptive, measured critique of the applicability of statistics to future events, see Blyth 2006; and for discussions of the related work of Nassim Taleb, see Blyth 2009, Jervis 2009, and Runde 2009.

5. Usually the models "cheat" by using survey data on presidential approval, survey data on the two candidates before and after their conventions, primary-election results, and other measures of voters' opinions about the presidential candidates, which are variants of the very thing expressed by their votes on Election Day. We already have plenty of polls, however; if the forecasting exercises have a scholarly purpose, it is to show that "real" factors, such as changes in unemployment rates and economic growth in a given quarter prior to the election, are (somehow) at work, even though the real factors alone cannot make accurate predictions, and so must be tweaked by using polls and other direct measures of opinion. The forecasters then fit various measures of public opinion and real factors against the small N of past presidential elections to produce a model that will forecast the next one, which presupposes that there is a temporally uniform underlying mélange of causes expressible in a formula weighting the various factors. The notion seems to be that as the N grows over time, the formulae will grow more precise overall, and that if they fail in a given case, that is only to be expected, as these are mere probability predictions. In short, only the inapplicability of the *ceteris paribus* clause, not the inapplicability of the *Homo economicus* model itself, is considered as a cause of outliers. See Campbell 2012 and 2013.

6. An interesting exception is explained in Lewis-Beck and Tien 2013. The authors' best-performing model in 2012 used only a measure of subjective perceptions of objective economic conditions: namely, the net proportion of survey respondents six months before the election who said that "business conditions are worse" than they had been previously. The authors explain that on the basis of "voter behavior theory," they would have preferred their old "Jobs Model" to the subjective model, but the predictions of the two models diverged, with the subjective model performing better (ibid., 39). That is, people's perceptions of economic conditions were more predictive of how they would vote than were the real conditions themselves. If so, however, then perhaps the dependent variable that should be of interest is not the electoral outcome (which we all find out, soon enough), but people's perceptions of

economic conditions; and perhaps the hypothesized independent variables should be factors (such as media coverage of economic conditions) that could produce these perceptions regardless of whether they accurately reflect real conditions. The election-forecasting scholarship is pointless curve fitting unless the models are supposed to identify what is *really* behind people's votes. But if this "real" factor is people's beliefs, then the economic factors used in the likes of the Jobs Model should be seen as, at best, proxies for what is actually causal: voter perceptions (whether of unemployment, business conditions, or anything else).

7. E.g., Fiorina 1981.
8. See n6 above.
9. Or they get washed out by the use of measures of opinion to diminish the impact of real factors alone; see n5 above.
10. Moreover, even if one votes out of a felt civic obligation rather than as an attempt to affect the outcome, this obligation is not fulfilled merely by voting per se. Few would claim that they have a civic obligation to show up at the polls but that, having done so, they may proceed to choose whom to vote for by flipping a coin. (How would such an obligation make sense?) Nor would an instrumentally rational voter who thought her vote was likely to be decisive have reason to try to affect the outcome (by voting) if she could not motivate a nonrandom vote. An obligation to vote, or a desire to affect the outcome, must entail voting for the "right" candidate, i.e., the one who, the voter predicts, is likely to advance what she takes to be good ends. Yet if people *knew*, as rational-ignorance theory holds, that they were too poorly informed to make such predictions with any reliability, because they had *deliberately* underinformed themselves, then they would have no reason, whether moral or instrumental, to vote.
11. A rejection of the pretense of predictive knowledge does not entail a rejection of determinism. I am suggesting that ideas are causes of behavior. In a Laplacean sense, one could, *in principle*, predict ideas, hence behavior, if one had omniscient command of all the antecedent conditions that lead one person to invent or endorse or transmit an idea, while another rejects it or never hears of it in the first place. However, we do not have such knowledge, and it is a safe bet that we never will. A predictive epistemology is logically possible but pragmatically impossible. The "laws" of epistemology may be knowable in principle, but not in practice.
12. Another path toward minimizing the role of subjective beliefs in human behavior is to treat emotions as overriding (rather than being triggered by) subjective beliefs, since emotions can be assumed to have some roughly general similarity across individuals, and these similarities can plausibly be seen as objective facts that directly control individual behavior. Long ago, Jervis (1976, 4–5) dispatched political psychologists' overemphasis on emotions by pointing out the performative contradiction it involves, at least if one is using emotion to explain the behavior of policy makers in non-crisis situations. The scholars attributing agents' behavior to emotion surely would not attribute their own attribution of emotion to the agents as the result of emotion. Cf. Friedman 2012 and Ross 2012.
13. This is not to say that there are no differences over values, any more than by bracketing the role of emotion, one is saying that emotion never overrides, rather than amplifying, rational judgment. But if one does not set values and

emotions to the side, one cannot even consider the possibility of subjective misperceptions of objective facts.

14. On complex-systems theories as theories about epistemology, not ontology, see McIntyre 1998.
15. Clearly, in this respect, I am departing from the letter of Jervis's book, but I hope not from the spirit.
16. I am referring to Hayek's quantitative notion of what makes "spontaneous" orders "complex phenomena." See Hayek 1967.
17. See Neumark and Wascher 2009 for summaries of many dozens of studies of the effects of minimum-wage increases.
18. In response to White House claims that "a range of economic studies show that modestly raising the minimum wage increases earnings and reduces poverty without measurably reducing employment," a *Wall Street Journal* editorial quoted David Neumark of the University of California at Irvine, who said that "the White House claim of de minimis job losses 'grossly misstates the weight of the evidence.' About 85 percent of the studies 'find a negative employment effect on low-skilled workers.'" "The Minority Youth Unemployment Act," *Wall Street Journal*, 19 February 2013.
19. Or, at best, putative known unknowns whose applicability Earle had reason to doubt.

REFERENCES

Blyth, Mark. 2006. "Great Punctuations: Prediction, Randomness, and the Evolution of Comparative Political Science." *American Political Science Review* 100(4): 493–98.

Blyth, Mark. 2009. "Coping with the Black Swan: The Unsettling World of Nassim Taleb." *Critical Review* 21(4): 447–65.

Campbell, James E. 2012. "Forecasting the 2012 American National Elections." *PS: Political Science and Politics* 45(4): 610–13.

Campbell, James E., ed., 2013. "Recap: Forecasting the 2012 Election." *PS: Political Science and Politics* 46(1): 37–48.

Converse, Philip E. 1964. "The Nature of Belief Systems in Mass Publics." In *Ideology and Discontent*, ed. David E. Apter. New York: Free Press.

Fiorina, Morris P. 1981. *Retrospective Voting in American National Elections*. New Haven: Yale University Press.

Friedman, Jeffrey. 2012. "Motivated Skepticism or Inevitable Conviction? Dogmatism in the Study of Politics." *Critical Review* 24(2): 131–55.

Friedman, Jeffrey, and Shterna Friedman, eds., 2012a. *The Nature of Belief Systems Reconsidered*. London: Routledge.

Friedman, Jeffrey, and Shterna Friedman, eds., 2012b. *Rethinking the Rhetorical Presidency*. London: Routledge.

Friedman, Jeffrey, and Shterna Friedman, eds., 2013. *Political Knowledge*, 4 vols. London: Routledge.

Friedman, Milton. 1953. "The Methodology of Positive Economics." In idem, *Essays on Positive Economics*. Chicago: University of Chicago Press.

Hayek, F. A. 1967. "The Theory of Complex Phenomena." In idem, *Studies in Philosophy, Politics, and Economics*. Chicago: University of Chicago Press.

Hetherington, Marc J. 1996. "The Media's Role in Forming Voters' National Economic Evaluations in 1992." *American Journal of Political Science* 40(2): 372–95. Republished in Friedman and Friedman 2013, vol. 3.

Holbrook, Thomas, and James C. Garand. 1996. "Homo Economicus? Economic Information and Economic Voting." *Political Research Quarterly* 49(2) (June): 351–75. Republished in Friedman and Friedman 2013, vol. 3.

Jervis, Robert. 1976. *Perception and Misperception in International Politics*. Princeton: Princeton University Press.

Jervis, Robert. 1997. *System Effects: Complexity in Political and Social Life*. Princeton: Princeton University Press.

Jervis, Robert. 2009. "Black Swans in Politics." *Critical Review* 21(4): 475–89.

Jervis, Robert. 2012. "System Effects Revisited." *Critical Review* 24(3): 393–415.

Jones-Rooy, Andrea, and Scott E. Page. 2012. "The Complexity of System Effects." *Critical Review* 24(3): 313–42.

Lewis-Beck, Michael S., and Charles Tien. 2013. "Proxy Forecasts: A Working Strategy." In Campbell 2013.

McIntyre, Lee. 1998. "Complexity: A Philosopher's Reflections." *Complexity* 3(6): 26–32.

Mitchell, Melanie. 2009. *Complexity: A Guided Tour*. New York: Oxford University Press.

Monteiro, Nuno. 2012. "We Can Never Study Merely One Thing: Reflections on Systems Thinking and IR." *Critical Review* 24(3): 343–66.

Monteiro, Nuno P., and Keven G. Ruby. 2009. "IR and the False Promise of Philosophical Foundations." *International Theory* 1(1): 15–48.

Neumark, David, and William L. Wascher. 2009. *Minimum Wages*. Cambridge, Mass: MIT Press.

Page, Scott E. 2011. *Diversity and Complexity*. Princeton: Princeton University Press.

Posner, Richard A. 2012. "Jervis on Complexity Theory." *Critical Review* 24(3): 367–73.

Ross, Lee. 2012. "Reflections on Biased Assimilation and Belief Polarization." *Critical Review* 24(2): 233–45.

Runde, Jochen. 2009. "Dissecting the Black Swan." *Critical Review* 21(4): 491–505.

Tetlock, Philip E. 2005. *Expert Political Judgment: How Good Is It? How Can We Know?* Princeton: Princeton University Press.

Tetlock, Philip E., Michael C. Horowitz, and Richard Herrmann. 2012. "Should 'Systems Thinkers' Accept the Limits on Political Forecasting or Push the Limits?" *Critical Review* 24(3): 375–91.

Tulis, Jeffrey. 1987. *The Rhetorical Presidency*. Princeton: Princeton University Press.

Ward, Michael D., and Nils Metternich. 2012. "Predicting the Future Is Easier than It Looks." *ForeignPolicy.com*, 23 November.

Weber, Max. [1904] 1949. "'Objectivity' in the Social Sciences." In idem, *The Methodology of the Social Sciences*, trans. Edward A. Shils and Henry A. Finch. New York: Free Press.

White, Wallace. 1989. "Her Deepness." *New Yorker*, 3 July: 41–65.

Andrea Jones-Rooy and Scott E. Page

THE COMPLEXITY OF SYSTEM EFFECTS

ABSTRACT: *Complexity science has witnessed a number of advances since the publication of Jervis's* System Effects. *These advances better allow us to untangle the messy elements in a system and predict sets of likely outcomes. However, just because a system is complex doesn't mean that all the ideas relating to complexity—such as agent-based modeling, path dependency, tipping points, between-class versus within-class effects, and networks—are necessarily relevant. One of our tasks is to determine whether they are—and, if so, their implications. As examples, we use China's role in the formation of the United States housing bubble; the federal government's bailout of AIG and Bear Stearns but not Lehman Brothers; and China's failure to experience a regime change such as the Middle East's Arab Spring.*

The decade and a half since the publication of Robert Jervis's *System Effects: Complexity in Political and Social Life* has been remarkable in many respects. We've witnessed the Arab Spring, the rise of China, the atrocities of September 11, the residential mortgage crisis in the United States, the global financial collapse, the euro crisis, the continued flattening of the global economy, and an increased awareness of climate change. Making sense of these events and trends requires thinking in terms of system effects, which, for Jervis, entails considering not only the

---

Andrea Jones-Rooy, Department of Social and Decision Sciences, Center for International Relations and Politics, Carnegie Mellon University, Pittsburgh, and Scott E. Page, Center for the Study of Complex Systems, Departments of Political Science and Economics, University of Michigan, thank Philip B. K. Potter, Kyle Joyce, Ken Kollman, and Jeffrey Friedman for comments on earlier versions. Research for this essay was funded by the U.S. Army Research Office.

strategic responses of actors to each other's anticipated actions, but also the effect that each action in a system has on the system as a whole.

A good example of system effects is the chain of events that led to the bursting of the housing bubble. The bubble developed because American households had access to cheap money. Debt was cheap because China pursued a strategy of growth based on exports. By discouraging domestic consumption and encouraging savings, China stockpiled the returns from its exports. In order to keep the price of its currency low and keep the dollar strong, China used these returns to buy American debt, which kept the cost of borrowing low for Americans and thus drove up housing prices (Casey 2012). Efforts to allow all Americans to share in the housing boom had the unintended systemic effect of creating a bubble, the bursting of which had enormous consequences. The residential mortgage crisis may have resulted from bankers' greed, poor checks and balances in granting loans, or naïve borrowers. But these causes were propelled by the systemic effects of an expansionist Chinese economic policy and by the efforts of the U.S. government to help people buy homes. Increased production of goods in China—and in Brazil, Russia, and India—also led to higher standards of living in those countries. However, it has also displaced jobs in industrialized countries and increased the level of atmospheric carbon, creating ever-greater concern about climate change.[1]

Thus, to paraphrase Jervis—the political, economic, social, and environmental worlds are systems. If we want to make sense of and improve these worlds, we need to understand how the systems affect each other. We need to explore both the boundaries of, and the connections between, systems.

This is no easy task. Understanding systems adequately would allow for better prediction, better political science, and better social science in general. No one (at least of note) predicted the Arab Spring, even though a few years earlier Stathis Kalyvas (1999) had called political science to task for not anticipating the overthrow of governments in the former Soviet Bloc. Similarly, only a handful of social scientists predicted the mortgage crisis or an event of the severity of September 11. Nor did social scientists twenty years ago consider the rise of China to be anything like a certainty.

In fairness, social scientists did correctly anticipate that climate change would become an important political issue, but they themselves may have contributed to making the issue salient. Nevertheless, since climate change is rife with system effects, scientists' predictions about its severity vary from mild to catastrophic. Naturally, these predictions are controversial. How worried should we be *right now*? We do not know for sure. But systems thinking is one of the most promising ways to further our understanding.[2]

Fortunately, advances in methodology have paralleled the increase in awareness of system effects since the publication of Jervis's book. Back then, the field of complex systems—the collection of theories that deal with system effects—was in its relative infancy. Underscoring Jervis's prescience, the study of complex systems has been transformed from a collection of related insights into a coherent discipline of study. Many of the ideas and concepts that Jervis introduced have, in the interim, received more formal treatments: to name just a few, phase transitions and tipping points (Jackson and Kollman 2010; Solé 2011; Lamberson and Page 2012), network effects (Newman 2010), path dependence (Page 2006; Pierson 2000), self-organized criticality (Bak 1996), and emergence (Bedau 1997; Holland 1998; Bedau and Humphreys 2008). "Complexity" itself is now much better defined. For example, several specific measures have been developed that explicitly measure how "complex" a system is.[3]

Despite the tremendous advances, we may remain ignorant of the future—or at least parts of it. Complex systems are, by definition, complex. They are comprised of many diverse, interdependent, and adaptive entities, the outcomes of which are difficult to predict (Page 2010). Even simple processes, such as repeatedly drawing a ball from an urn (more on this in the next section), contain an element of complexity, where anything can happen. By this definition, then, whatever happens will be surprising and unpredictable.

This is not to say that complex systems are always completely unwieldy. It is possible for the set of possible outcomes in some systems to be small enough for us to predict outcomes accurately. Other times, however, even in these seemingly more straightforward systems, the results may run counter to our predictions.

This leads to three important points. First, systems can produce either complexity or order (such as static equilibrium or periodicity). One reason to construct models of systems is to gain a foothold on the *type* of outcome that is likely to occur rather than to predict a specific outcome. Will the outcome be complex or simple? Will it be predictable? This information alone can get us a long way toward understanding a given system.

The second point is that not everything is a system and not everything is complex. While systems are prevalent, they are not everywhere. And one must resist the temptation to cast all phenomena in terms of either systems or complexity. Thus, yet another reason to construct systems models of social life is to find out whether a given process or outcome is indeed part of a system or the result of one.

Finally, complex processes often defy specific prediction not only because of their inherent contingency, but also because our information—and our powers of inference—may be limited. Thus, while we may be unable to predict the outcomes of some complex systems, *ex post* we can make sense of them. In such contexts, tools from complexity science can help us to reconstruct the past with greater accuracy, i.e., to identify the actual causal forces (Watts 2011). This emphasis on qualitatively chasing causal arrows is different from the emphasis of many social scientists, as it lies between the thick description that tends to come from careful qualitative work, and the shallower but more generalizable explanations that come from quantitative work. All three methods—qualitative, quantitative, and this *in-between*—are valuable, but the in-between has thus far been the most neglected by social scientists.

Before we continue, we have one important point of distinction to make. Jervis refers to *systems*, whereas we will refer to *complex systems*. Complex systems consist of diverse, interdependent, interacting entities whose aggregate behaviors can often transcend the characteristics of the parts. Complex systems include not only political and economic systems but also the brain and ecological systems.

When Jervis speaks of system effects, he means two things: the interdependencies between actions—how one actor's choices affect another's choices—and emergent properties, which is how micro-level actions produce (intentionally or otherwise) macro-level behaviors that in turn influence the system. China's loaning money to the United States, sustaining U.S. indebtedness, is an example of interdependency; climate change is an example of an emergent property.

Interdependencies can be captured in system dynamics models (Sterman 2000), which focus on interactions between variables. Emergent effects are more commonly found in bottom-up complex systems models, which assume interacting agents. In either framework, system effects can produce complexity—phenomena that are difficult to describe, engineer, or predict (Page 2010)—but they can also produce equilibria, chaos, or simple periodic patterns. In *A New Kind of Science*, the physicist Stephen Wolfram (2002) showed how simple rule-based systems can produce all four of these kinds of outcomes.

In the remainder of this paper we will discuss several advances in complex-systems research, such as path dependence, tipping points, and network effects. We then consider how thinking in terms of system effects provides a new lens through which to view China, and we analyze whether it may experience a "Chinese Spring" similar to the Arab Spring. Our aim will be not to give definitive accounts or predict the future, but to highlight the importance of system effects. Finally, we examine how systems thinking might advance the study of political and economic systems.

The Foundations of System Effects

In *System Effects* Jervis pointed out that events at the macro level need not align with motivations at the micro level, and he emphasized that outcomes in one domain can have systemic effects in other domains.[4] These two observations form the core of any inquiry into a complex system.

It is one thing to observe that macro outcomes and systemic effects matter and resonate with our understanding of the world. It is another to be able to do something about it. Jervis's book was far ahead of its time. When it was published, complex systems theorists did not have, as they do now, an extensive number of conceptual and research tools. Since then, the concepts of emergence, tipping points, path dependence, network effects, and even complexity itself have been formalized. The field of systems dynamics has also seen advances (Sterman 2000) and has become a mainstream part of graduate curricula in schools of management and natural resources. Unfortunately, neither complex systems nor systems dynamics have yet become mainstream in political science (de Marchi 2005).

Within the social sciences at large, however, several important components of complex systems—networks, interdependencies, adaptation, and heterogeneity—have become more central (Miller and Page 2007). Many studies, for example, have made use of network analyses of human behavior (Christakis and Fowler 2009). Others have focused on the role of diverse elements in producing complex outcomes (Page 2007 and 2010). Yet the inclusion of these components in social science analyses has not yet led to the consideration of complex systems as a whole. Some political-science research, for example, has incorporated network effects, but they comprise only a small portion of systems theory. The focus on network effects provides only a partial view of complex systems.

Agent-based modeling is a central methodological tool in the study of complex systems in full. Yet since their introduction, the use of agent-based models to explore those systems has not been as widespread as might have been expected. There are many excellent exceptions: Cederman 1997, Lustick and Miodownik 2000, Bhavnani 2003, and Joyce 2012 use agent-based models to analyze coalitions, conflict, and uprising. Axelrod 1997 and Bednar et al. 2010 explore the formation and persistence of distinct yet diverse cultures.[5] Laver 2005 and 2007 use agent-based models to illuminate how candidates position themselves in democratic elections. And Hausmann and Hidalgo 2009 shows how complexity theory can help us understand economic growth by considering not only aggregate data but types of industries. These examples notwithstanding, agent-based modeling has not yet become mainstream in any of the social sciences.

The advances in complexity research and systems theory rely on both mathematical and agent-based models. Mathematical models are widespread in many fields of social science, including Jervis's home field, international relations. Mathematical models rely on proofs, while agent-based models rely on computation, but the differences between mathematical or game-theoretic models and agent-based models are not as extreme as many believe (Epstein 2006; Kollman 2012). Both rely on the explicit construction of purposive actors and aggregate the behavior of those actors. Further, both focus on the resulting outcome, which can be any of the four kinds outlined by Wolfram (2002). Perhaps most importantly, both types of model allow for strategic behavior by actors.

Typically in game-theoretic models, two or three players face off in a strategic situation: Each anticipate what the others will do and choose actions accordingly. In agent-based models, agents (actors) also take into account the actions of others in the system, be they neighbors, similar agents, agents without much in common with themselves, or even all agents—or they can pick actions at random. The strategic interactions in agent-based models can give rise to important outcomes, such as the emergence of a cooperative society, or of distinct clusters of agents whose attributes or behaviors may be similar or may diverge widely from one another (Axelrod 1985 and 1997; Bednar et al. 2010).

How one tests models of either type has been the subject of debate. Both Scott de Marchi (2005) and Keven A. Clarke and David M. Primo (2012) criticize the approach to social science that solves for equilibrium and then runs a regression based on the comparative statics, but they do so for different reasons. De Marchi points to the fact that, given the abundance of plausible and similar models, game-theoretic models based on a particular functional form may not tell us more than we already know. Clarke and Primo, on the other hand, highlight the mismatch between assumptions in the theoretical and the empirical models, which calls into question how much one can claim from an empirical test.

The study of complex systems has advanced our understanding of many topics that play prominent roles in Jervis's book, but we will focus on the three that can be most readily applied to current social-scientific work: path dependence, tipping points, and networks.

Path Dependence

In its crudest form, "path dependence" means that history matters. The concept was formalized by Paul A. David (1994 and 2007) and Brian Arthur (1994). Both David and Arthur relied on the Polya process, which refers to a scenario where an urn contains balls of two colors. Each time a ball is selected, another ball of the same color is placed in the urn. This particular type of "increasing returns" produces two surprising results. First, any distribution across the two colors is possible and equally likely to occur. Second, any series of outcomes of the first color is as likely as the series of outcomes of the other color. Suppose the two colors are red and blue. In ten draws, getting six reds followed by four blues has the same probability of occurring as drawing two reds and then alternating blues and reds over the next eight draws. This means that, at least in this abstract example, at the beginning of any history, we have no way of knowing which path is more or less likely.

Why does this matter? Paul Pierson (2000 and 2004) and Jervis both discuss the prevalence of increasing returns and path-dependent outcomes in systems. This contingency lies at the core of Jervis's argument. If what happens depends on what occurs along the way, then the world becomes less predictable than linear thinking would suggest. This leaves us with a bit of a problem from a scientific perspective: How can we make predictions in a world where slight aberrations today might change the path tremendously down the road? Is everything contingent? Acknowledging the "butterfly effect" can make forecasters throw up their hands when it comes to making predictions about the social world.

Happily, since the publication of Jervis's book, the concept of path dependence and its relationship to increasing returns have become better understood. Most importantly, we can unpack exactly what path dependence means. First, Page 2006 shows that increasing returns are neither necessary nor sufficient for path dependence. Increasing returns may produce path dependence, but other things may, too. Moreover, a system can exhibit increasing returns but not be path dependent or it can be path dependent but not exhibit increasing returns. Most important for Jervis's argument, Page 2006 shows that externalities and interdependencies often produce path dependence. Therefore, outcomes may be more contingent than Jervis assumed. Unfortunately, testing for path dependence proves harder than are might think (Jackson and Kollman 2010).

Understanding the distinction between path-dependent outcomes and path-dependent equilibria is crucial to identifying path dependence in data. Systems can produce path-dependent outcomes—that is, what matters in the next moment depends on what happened up to that point—even while failing to exhibit path-dependent equilibria—where what happens in the long run does not depend on the path of outcomes. In other words, it may not matter that many paths to a given end could have been taken. For example, the fact that the United States expanded steadily westward to span both coasts of the North American continent can be seen as path dependent, yet if Americans had settled in New England, then the Pacific Northwest, then the South, then California, then the Midwest, the current outcome would likely look the same.

If anything, the fact that all outcomes are not path dependent reinforces Jervis's argument. First, if we see contingent behavior—not just increasing returns, but any type of interdependent behavior—then we should look for path dependence. Thus, path-dependent outcomes may be even more ubiquitous than Jervis claims. Second, the fact that outcomes can be path dependent but that long-run equilibria need not be means we need deeper thinking and better models. Scholars cannot merely identify contingent outcomes and infer that the system will produce path dependency. These more formal definitions help us measure and empirically identify path dependence, and they help advance social science as it moves beyond isolated examples and metaphors to the analysis of data.

Tipping Points

Jervis notes that systems with feedbacks and interdependent behavior can often "tip," that is, small events or changes in the environment can result in large changes in the systems. The term *tipping point* has, of course, entered the common vernacular due to Malcolm Gladwell's best-selling book of that title and Davis Guggenheim's Oscar-winning documentary, *Earth in the Balance*, which describes how the earth's climate may be nearing a tipping point. The concept has been used to describe phenomena as diverse as the Arab Spring and the rise of Facebook, but this tendency to identify any large event as a tipping point runs counter to the agenda that Jervis lays out. Understanding system effects enables us to determine which types of systems might be prone (or not) to tips. Ideally, this would enable us to prevent undesirable tips and to encourage beneficial ones. To meet these goals, we need to understand systems more deeply and learn what causes tipping points.

Mathematicians rarely refer to "tipping points." Instead, they distinguish types of tipping points. For example, "unstable equilibria" refers to the points in a system at which any small perturbation will cause the system to move. Many of the social-scientific examples of tipping points are unstable equilibria. "Bifurcation" describes a change from a single stable point to something else, perhaps a cycle due to a small change in a parameter. Physicists, relatedly, describe "phase transitions" (Solé 2011), in which the behavior of an entire system changes due to a small change in some parameter.

As in the case of path dependence, these formal definitions and results provide common precise definitions, allow for the derivation of mathematical results, and enable empirical work. But to do so, these ideas from mathematics and physics must be translated into the language and contexts that concern social science. Lamberson and Page 2012 categorizes these various types of tips along two dimensions. Tips can be direct, with an action begetting more of that same action, such as when one rioter induces others to join. Tips can also be contextual, where the environment changes in some small way so that existing behavior aggregates very differently, such as in epidemiology, where small changes in virulence or connectedness can lead to epidemics.

Some examples may help clarify the relevance of the distinctions. Imagine a three-candidate majority-rule election in which a conservative candidate is getting forty percent of the vote in polls and each of the liberal candidates earns about thirty percent. This might be an unstable equilibrium: As soon as one liberal candidate gets a slight lead, other liberal voters may switch their vote to her. This means the system might tip so that she ultimately gets a majority of the vote. In this example, a few trembles to the system directly cause it to tip. Contrast this with changes in technology that allow for better communication among protestors. This may enable mass uprisings that previously had been impossible to organize. In this instance, the context changes, which allows almost any action to result in a tip. A small change in a parameter—the connectedness of society—drives the tip.

Lamberson and Page also distinguish within-class from between-class tips. This distinction relies on Wolfram's classification of systems outcomes as being of one of four types—equilibrium, periodic, random, or complex. A within-class tip occurs when a system tips to a new outcome but the class of outcome stays the same. If a market moves from one equilibrium to another, the system has tipped within class. Alternatively, a system can tip between classes. In the Arab Spring, societies tipped from relative equilibrium to what would best be called "complex." Since then, Tunisia has settled into something of a new equilibrium, Egypt and Libya remain complex, and Syria is complex but edging into chaos.[6]

This framework enables us to better categorize and understand tips and to recognize that not all dramatic increases result from tips. Consider first, the rise of Facebook. Figure 1 shows a sharp increase in the number of Facebook users, but that was not a tip. It was the natural result of an exponential growth process, like an epidemic. In contrast, tipping points are specific actions or changes in the environment that result in dramatically different outcomes.

Contrast Facebook's rise with the Arab Spring. In the latter, singular events led to uprisings, but probably less because of the events themselves and more because the context had changed. In Tunisia in 2010 it was not obvious at the outset that an action by a single man in a city square would lead to the overthrow of a regime, much less be heralded as the beginning of a cascade of uprisings around the Middle East. We can say

Figure 1. Growth in Number of Facebook Users

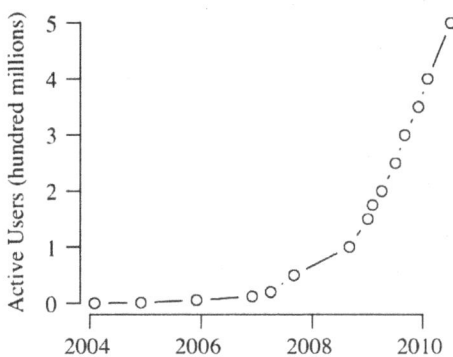

Source: Lamberson and Page 2012

now that this single event may have sparked the uprising, but for something to be a cause, it has to take place in a context that is ripe for it to generate effects. There have been more than forty self-immolations in Tibet since 2009, yet they have not had anything like the effects of one self-immolation in Tunisia.

Some points to keep in mind, then, are that tipping points are not identifiable by abrupt changes in value. Moreover, while they require an action to get underway, it could be that almost any action will do once the context has tipped. Finally, tipping points imply abrupt changes in the distribution over outcomes, but the changes need not necessarily be immediate. Therefore, to identify tipping points, we cannot just look at time series and seek out kinks. We need to know not only the current state of the world, but also where it is headed.

Networks

System effects can occur at the macro level, such as when greater demand for some commodity leads to an increase in its price, which thereby reduces demand for it. They can also spread through networks, in which one's predisposition to engage in some activity depends on the actions of one's network of friends. The study of networks has made tremendous advances over the past fifteen years. Scholars now study networks at three levels: formation (or logic), structure, and function (Newman 2010). Most networks form through decentralized individual actions:

individuals make friends, power companies build lines, firms sign contracts with one another, and countries form alliances and make trade agreements.

The accumulation of these rules results in a structure.[7] A network can be characterized by an average degree, which is the mean number of connections ("edges" in networks parlance) for every point in the network (each "node"). It can also be characterized by the distribution over those degrees. Networks also have clustering coefficients, which are the likelihood that B and C are connected if A is connected to both B and C. They also have path lengths, the average number of links that must be traversed to get from one node to another. These network statistics

Figure 2. Co-Risk Among Financial Institutions

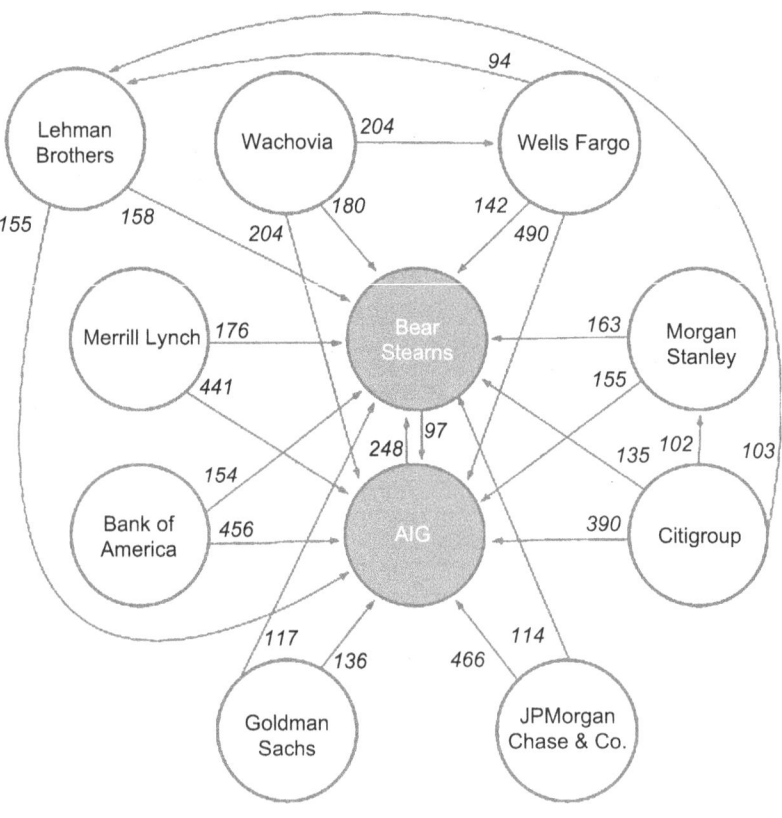

Source: IMF 2009, Figure 2.6

capture variations in structure. Scholars have been able to use these measures to show how social networks differ from citation networks and networks of neurons in the brain. In the future, they might also be able to help social scientists distinguish stable societies from unstable ones.

Network structure merits attention because it has implications for understanding system effects (Maoz 2010). Figure 2 shows the co-risk for various financial institutions. Co-risk can be thought of as the extent to which a bad event for one institution will affect institutions with which it trades. Larger numbers mean more risk. The numbers in Figure 2 were estimated prior to the collapse of Lehman Brothers and the bailout of AIG.

Banks trading with one another were primarily interested not in the robustness of the overall network, but in making money. The network structure of co-risk emerged from that logic of formation. Policy makers, however, were interested in how the network would function. Particularly, would it survive the failure of Bear Stearns, AIG, or Lehman Brothers? Figure 2 shows that the systemic effects of an AIG failure would have been much larger than a failure by Lehman Brothers, with Bear Stearns lying somewhere in between, which accords with how the government saw it, too. And it took appropriate action (by bailing out AIG, facilitating a buyout of Bear Stearns, but letting Lehman Brothers collapse).[8]

Networks can also be used more qualitatively to capture system effects. Figure 3 illustrates how one can map the complexity of a network. The figure is loosely based on a proprietary network map that was developed by a consulting firm for use by the U.S. government in Afghanistan. Each of the seven displayed clusters of actors or outcomes (originally there were twelve) describes a very broad category of actor or condition (e.g., "insurgents," "coalition domestic support," "government capacity," "infrastructure services," "Afghan National Security Forces" [ANSF]). Clustered around these rubrics were a total of 110 nodes connected by arrows: For example, the node labeled "perception of government strength" had arrows indicating that it contributed, among other things, to "private sector workforce," which in turn contributed to "civilian services," which in turn contributed to the fulfillment of "population basic needs," which in turn contributed to "visible gains in security," which in turn contributed to "satisfaction with gains in security"—which, in turn, led back to "perception of government strength." The network is complex, but an analyst can look

Figure 3. The Many Interacting Factors in a Complex Network

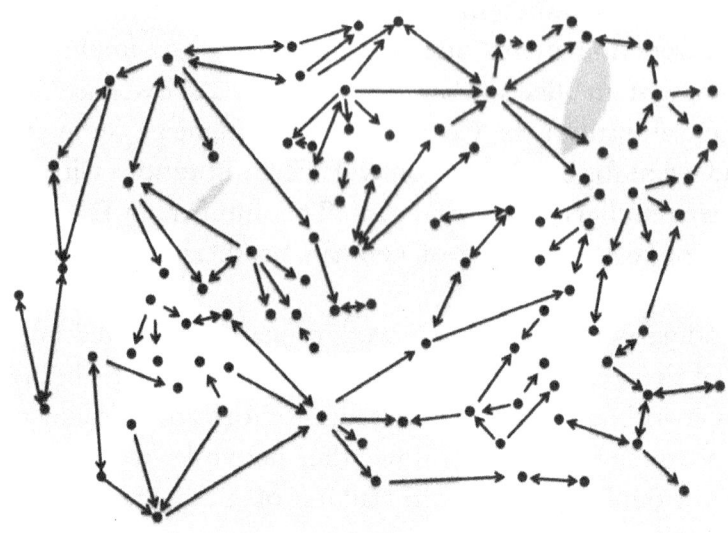

at individual nodes and follow the system effects of a policy choice. While the relative magnitude of those effects may be difficult to disentangle, their signs can be relevant in helping to guide resources into areas with larger positive feedbacks. For example, three individually compelling allocations of funds might all eventually lead to increased power to the insurgents. Budgeting could then steer clear of those traps or even fund countervailing alternatives.

This type of graph can be used to portray any type of complex system. For example, it can illustrate the complexities in the U.S. housing market by having various clusters represent increased savings in China, the expansion of home ownership in the United States, the growth in low-income mortgages, and poor checks and balances. The connecting nodes might then point to the outcome of an inflated American housing market.

In complex systems, an individual action can have multiple consequences (pleiotrapy) and be influenced by multiple other actions (epistasis). In the long run, almost everything affects everything, and while this kind of claim does not seem very scientific at first glance, it does not mean that it is incorrect or even useless. Being aware of the many cascading effects of a particular policy choice can mean more effective policymaking with fewer unintended outcomes.

We cannot know a priori which element in the networks might change first and cause a major contextual change—or a tip. The more connections a particular element has with other elements, for example, the more likely that a change to it will have systemic effects. Thus, we can approximate system effects by using approximations of networks to guide policy decisions.

The Systemic Effects of China

China's economic rise since the beginning of its Open Door Policy in 1979, and especially during the last fifteen years, has resulted from investments in interdependent activities. Increased trade with Europe and the United States, urbanization, increased tourism flowing into and out of the country, privatization of industry, and a large workforce, among myriad other factors, have all contributed to an explosion in economic growth. With that growth has come a rise in political status. China now holds sway in many international organizations, especially regional ones such as the Association of Southeast Asian Nations. China's economic growth has also increased its need for energy resources. It has thus developed stronger ties to Africa and the Middle East, bringing further political and social influence to these regions and—due to the strategic importance of these regions—the global system.

China's energy demands have also driven investment in new technologies, including solar and wind power. Here again we see a system effect: Energy demands drive technological development, which in turn requires investment in education. Philip B. K. Potter (2012) argues that this increased interconnectedness also increases the risks to China of terrorism, especially emanating from movements toward Xinjiang separatism.

Finally, environmentally, China's economic rise could not be more influential from a systems perspective. Air pollution generated in China finds its way across the Pacific to the coast of California—an obvious example of actors in a system affecting other actors. China's tremendous growth in industry and infrastructure generates greenhouse gases and other potentially climate-disrupting elements. China's farming practices, population size, and the expanding affluent class, with its attendant needs (such as cars), have tremendous environmental implications. Most household water in China is not potable, so the Chinese purchase vast numbers of plastic water bottles, which require energy to produce and dispose of. The large population's need for chopsticks requires wood and thus affects forests. Environmental effects reverberate through complex systems (for example, ecosystems), making it nearly impossible to predict outcomes of any of these changes without a systems approach.

China's sheer size is also a factor. If Germany or the United States significantly reduced its automobile emissions or coal consumption, the global benefits could be slight given the rate of emission growth in China. Of course, China, Europe, and the United States are not the only players in this environmental system: The BRIC countries, in particular, but also the growing populations and economies in South Africa, Nigeria, Turkey, the UAE, and many others generate more pressure on existing environmental resources while simultaneously contaminating the air, water, and food supply. The structure of the network, the size of an actor in it, and the magnitude and direction of the influence between two actors can change how information, disease, or policy can spread across it.

China's increased role in the international system poses challenges, but it may also offer solutions. While China's continued economic growth is far from guaranteed, the fact that China has thus for been able to weather the economic storm in Europe, means that China could be a force for economic resilience in the future. Growth in China's science and industry can lead to medical innovations, cures for diseases, natural-disaster response teams, and, more generally, the opportunity to spread positive influence around the world. More educated Chinese citizens means more people ready to help tackle the next generation of global problems. These claims are speculative, but we wish to emphasize that systems can have both good and bad effects. Most likely the global impact of the rise of China will lie somewhere between a total disaster and the salvation of humanity, but that's a pretty large gray area. Yet advances in complex systems can help us be more specific.

Path Dependence in China

Was China's rise inevitable? Is China on a path to global dominance? A naïve way to think about China's growth would be to invoke the notion of increasing returns at the metaphorical level: The more we see of something, the more likely we are to see more of it. Thus, urbanization begat more urbanization, exports have driven exports, and so on. This logic does not get us far: What were the mechanisms behind increasing returns from urbanization and exports? Which elements were subject to increasing returns, and when were other factors at play?

Increasing returns rely on the logic of positive feedback, but attributing China's economic growth to increasing returns does not tell us very much. China's rise can also be attributed to micro-level factors, although that does not mean ditching "external" factors, such as trade competition. Nothing is truly external in a system; there are only elements that are less or more connected to others. Micro-level factors may have been set in motion by self-reinforcement or lock-in, meaning that a single choice or action by the Chinese government, such as the 1979 Open Door Policy, set into place incentives for the development of other "complementary institutions that encourage[d] that choice to be sustained" (Page 2006, 88). This is the logic to which many China historians may be most attracted, although we don't know of any systemic analysis to evaluate which path-dependent process, if any, best explains China's economic growth. Such an analysis would take into account specific industries and technologies that have contributed to growth, which of course also depends on the constellation of investments, i.e. interdependencies, as well as the actions of neighboring countries (Hausmann and Hidalgo 2009). This explicit consideration of industry-level investments can give us a much better understanding of path contingency. In particular, some investments—such as investments in capital markets—may have been necessary in order to hold the system together. The Chinese government may have benefitted from investing in building large factories in rural China when more local entrepreneurs did so, too. A series of foreign direct investors in China may then have seen their investments grow as more investors followed suit.

Such detailed accounts are in sharp contrast with a casual "history matters" increasing-returns perspective, which might abstractly acknowledges that China's current and future economic state depends on its past. However, this acknowledgment is trivial and empty, both as explanation and prediction. It is concerned with what Page (2006, 89) calls "phat" dependence, where only the set of outcomes (not how one arrives at it) matters.

While China's economy is increasingly free compared to its former command economy, the Chinese government still has tremendous influence over the planning and management of many key elements. The government tends to choose where to locate particular firms or industries and, in doing so, it may be less concerned with the potential efficiency gains of putting technologically innovative firms in the same place and more concerned with demographics, wealth distribution, transportation needs or constraints, and space and labor force needs or constraints.[9] A purported advantage of China's political and economic system is that its insulation from the electorate allows for longer planning horizons. This means that China should, through this planning, be able to avoid inefficient path dependencies—such as the cumbersome healthcare programs passed in the United States.

But that does not free China from phat or path dependence; it means only that there might be less lock-in than in other countries, as China can step out of non-productive paths without worrying about voter disapproval. There should be less room for historical accidents. While this is in contrast to the historical contingencies (rather than plans of a central organizer) that led, say, to the explosive growth of industry in Silicon Valley (Arthur 1994), there is, of course, still room for contingencies. First, provincial decentralization and increased activism by Chinese citizens limit the extent to which China's leadership can truly guide its economic path. Furthermore, even if China's control over the economy were absolute, an event or accident could lead it in an unanticipated direction. For example, the Chinese government's investment in a particular industry in a particular region could encourage the development of auxiliary industries, which would lead to path dependence in these related industries. Thus, the Chinese government may be effective at anticipating and thus minimizing certain types of path dependence, but it cannot prevent the introduction of unforeseeable paths.

China in the International System

China's economic growth may stem not simply from the endogenous factors we considered above, but from exogenous factors, too, since "everything else will not [ever] remain constant" (Jervis 1997, 7). A systems perspective suggests that even if China had followed the same national economic policies, its growth would have been different in a different global environment. As Jervis emphasizes, both system and actor characteristics matter in explaining outcomes—at the level of both the system and the actor. In this way, Jervis's argument is compatible with constructivist ideas in international relations that center on interactions between the actor and the system. What China does affects where China ends up; what else is happening in the international system should also affect where China ends up; and, most importantly from a systems perspective, what China does affects the system, which affects where China ends up, which affects what China does, which affects the system, which affects China, and so on. Add to this the fact that the same process is true for all actors in the system—the United States, Europe, India, Al Qaeda, Enron, etc.—and we have a seemingly intractable tangle of inextricable factors.

How does one get a handle on such issues? The beauty of complex systems is that while they are difficult to predict at levels of pinpoint accuracy, they are also not random. It is possible to find patterns in the mess and understand the underlying individual incentives that give rise to those patterns. Just because we do not know what will happen ten years from now does not mean we cannot point to salient relationships and interconnections and form a general expectation about how factors might interact and which phenomena will emerge from them. Agent-based modeling (de Marchi 2005; Miller and Page 2007), for example, enables us to construct artificial worlds with many interdependent actors, and allows us to compare models based on different scenarios to predict which outcomes are most likely.

Tipping Points

Will the political or economic growth of China cause the international system to "tip" into something new? Will the growth of industry and automobile use in China lead to an environmental tip where we have serious and sudden, unexpected climate changes? Might there even be some kind of social tip of China's influence over the international system?

It is tempting to overuse the idea of a tipping point. It is more analytically satisfying and fruitful to break the idea down into a number of different possible processes that might lead a system to change in some way. This helps us determine what is truly a tip—that is, how do we know if the system has changed in some deep way, as opposed to it becoming only superficially different?—and to determine, as well, the underlying cause of the change. Consider the difference between unstable equilibria, bifurcations, and phase transitions. If the international political system is currently at an unstable equilibrium, then any minor further shift upward in China's political power should cause the system to change. If that's the case, then we should closely watch for shifts in China's political or economic influence. If the system is not at an unstable equilibrium, then we don't need to worry. But it is more likely that China is headed towards contextual change that will enable further change than that it is poised at some unstable point.[10]

We can also apply the logic of types of tips to understanding China's economic and political growth in the international system. One example of a direct tip is China's investments in Angola, Nigeria, South Africa, and other resource-rich African countries. China's investments may spur other countries to invest there, too. A contextual tip, on the other hand, might result from the same activity: As China's resource-extraction activities in Africa increase, a shift in the global climate may cause the deleterious effects of this extraction to expand, too. In both the direct and contextual cases, the outcome is negative environmental consequences as a result of extraction, but the reasons are very different.

In addition to direct and contextual tips, there are also within-class and between-class tips. If China's economic growth, for example, were likely to give rise to a within-class tip, this would mean that the system might shift from one equilibrium to another, or from one complex dynamic to another. If China's growth were to lead to a between-class tip, it would shift the system from, for example, an equilibrium to a periodic system. Distinguishing between these tips allows us to adjust policies accordingly.

We can apply the logic of tipping points not just to phenomena in the international system, but also to systems within China (or any country, society, or group). For example, why hasn't China "tipped" into a democracy? The events in Tiananmen Square in 1989 came closest to being a potential tipping point in China. In other countries, such as those in Eastern Europe at the same time, protests of that magnitude led to regime-wide tips. In recent years protests in China have increased in response to issues as varied as government control, corruption, and anti-Japan, anti-Taiwan, or anti-American sentiments. Other forms of disruptions, such as mass suicides to protest factory conditions, have also taken place.

In 1997 in Gulja, a city in Xinjiang province, protestors took to the streets to protest the recent execution of several independence activists and to indicate their desire for independence. After two days the Chinese government used violence to shut down the protests. Official records show that nine citizens were killed, but the number may in fact be much higher. This event could well have tipped a regime in another context. Tunisia's 2010–11 "tip" (see the next section) can be traced to just one man. Why didn't this happen in China? Is China especially good at cutting off protests before they grow too large?

For a direct tip to occur, one of two things would have to take place. Either the system would have to be at an unstable equilibrium, where one action would set in motion a sequence of responses that lead to a drastic systemic change, or the system would have previously had to have undergone a contextual tip, where increased connectedness or frustration entails that responses that in the past would have created only small ripples now spread quickly across the social landscape.

Let us consider the latter possibility—a contextual change that enables unrest to spread more easily. This is a plausible scenario in the future, but has some factor, or collection of factors, prevented such a contextual change from happening in China already?

The Chinese government has every incentive to prevent contextual changes, such as increased connectedness or citizen dissatisfaction, so as to prevent a political tipping point from being reached. The government may be working actively to ensure that precisely such a contextual change will not take place, using, in particular, the national media. The media in China are, of course, censored (King, Pan, and Roberts 2012). Scholars and policy makers are interested in determining the extent and criteria of the censorship: What is the logic by which the government chooses to publish a news story? Uncontrolled media might be able to increase connectedness by, say, publishing stories that will outrage readers, leading them to seek out like-minded and similarly angry citizens. But the strongest effect of the media may be their ability to influence citizens' level of satisfaction with the regime. This is determined, in large part, by which news stories are selected for dissemination.

Ideally, from the perspective of the government, the media in China could be completely controlled by being prohibited from publishing or broadcasting troubling news stories, allowing only flattering ones to circulate. In reality, however, the government does not have perfect control. Information flows into the country through a variety of means that the government cannot completely monitor: emails, letters, and phone calls from members of the Chinese Diaspora into China; news brought by foreigners visiting China; and such websites as Weibo, China's most popular version of Twitter, which greatly accelerates the flow of this new information throughout China. According to the *New York Times*, even totalitarian North Korea cannot completely stop the trickle of outside information that "contaminates" its propaganda environment (Sang-Hun 2012).

In light of this fact, Jones-Rooy 2012a contends that the Chinese government balances the need to keep the national media credible against a desire to maintain regime legitimacy by highlighting "good" news stories and burying or blocking "bad" ones. In an era that sees information leaks about any major event, domestic or international, the government cannot be caught not reporting them, lest it lose the trust of its citizens. Media that are controlled but that everyone knows to be controlled undermines control. Indeed, the more likely the citizens are to find out about a particular event, however unflattering it is to the regime, the more likely the Chinese government has been willing to publish the story, despite risks to its legitimacy. The potential cost in lost credibility of doing otherwise is too high.

The media exemplify how the Chinese government walks a careful path to prevent changes in the context that might allow a political tip. While it is intuitive to think that the government should not want to make citizens angry if its interest is in social stability, a formal understanding of tipping points allows us to recognize that tips require a contextual shift that would allow sparks to ignite, instead of flaring momentarily and dying out.

The major impediments to applying such an analysis routinely are that it is, admittedly, not easy to do, and that scholars of complex systems and international relations have not been collaborating. An increase in the frequency of collaboration—particularly between scholars in the fields of complex systems and international relations—should help make the use of advances in the study of system effects more standard practice.

Networks

The concept of networks is one of the major advances in the study of complex systems and the one most widely applied in political-science research thus far. This is not surprising: Networks are created when actors influence each other, whether technologically, economically, socially, epidemiologically, or politically. International trade represents a network, as might the flow of information about trade.

However, while networks are widespread, not all outcomes we see are network effects. For example, the literature on policy diffusion in American politics describes the adoption of policies by different U.S. states, a process that might look like one of influence spreading across networks. Instead, this area of research identifies four major mechanisms of policy diffusion: emulation; learning (where a state builds upon or varies an existing policy); competition to respond to a change in the system; and coercion (the federal government requires all states to adopt the same policy) (Shipan and Volden 2008). We may be tempted to tell a networks story, whereby one state adopts a policy and communicates its benefits or techniques to neighboring or otherwise connected states, but this has not been found to be one of the prominent mechanisms by which policies are diffused in the United States.

Similarly, in the international system, we may be tempted to label as network effects the spread of states signing international treaties, adopting particular voting rules, or adopting stringent environmental policies. But it is not always easy to tell whether the apparent "spread" of a phenomenon is due to a network effect or some other underlying process. Jervis (1997, 26) addresses this issue when he asks, "Was 1968 a turbulent year in some countries because there had been disturbances in others, or were an unusual number of societies independently unstable, perhaps because they were feeling the same tensions?"

In the case of China, knowing whether a particular issue is subject to network effects is a first step toward understanding the kind of influence China may have. The second step, if there is a possibility of a network effect, is understanding the network—that is, focusing on the structure of the network, the number of nodes, the degree and distribution of edges, etc. For example, how should we view China's increasing investment in African countries? Is it—as many analysts and policy makers in the energy market worry—snapping up resources and making them unavailable to other countries? What if one of the resource host countries abruptly decides to block China's access? And does China's trade with Iran undermine the United States and other countries' political efforts to influence Iran through an embargo?

Knowing whether there is a network in the international oil market and, if so, what kind, are first steps toward answering this question. Figure 4 presents data on the top ten international oil exporters and importers as of 2008. There are several things to note. First, many countries (those at the perimeter of the graph) rely on just 2–4 supplier countries for oil. Second, most oil exporters export to many countries, not just a few. Third, China and the United States both appear at the center of the network, importing from many different suppliers. It is beyond our current scope to conduct extensive network analysis of this graph, but it would be relatively straightforward to evaluate the robustness of this network to various kinds of shocks. And one can then ask further questions, such as how China's growing demand for other resources besides oil might affect the network. This type of exercise has become part of network-analysts' tool kit and has been applied to questions regarding the robustness of the Internet, electric power grids, and ecosystems (see Callaway et al. 2000).

Putting It All Together: The Arab Spring vs. the Rise of China

The events in 2010 that culminated in the Arab Spring were in no way predictable. With the benefit of hindsight, it is tempting to tell a simple causal story: The actions of a single man in Tunisia led to a regime overthrow, which led to the Arab Spring. This story begs many questions: How inevitable was the overthrow of Tunisia's government in the first days of the uprising events? Were analysts worried in October and November 2010 about what might happen in Tunisia? Why were the uprisings as big as they were? Why did they succeed (in the case of Tunisia)? Why did they spread to other Middle Eastern countries? Why did they not spread beyond the Middle East?

The events of the Arab Spring represent path-dependent outcomes. Were the events path-dependent equilibria, i.e., phat dependent? Would the Arab Spring have looked at all the same had it begun, say, in Syria and then spread to Tunisia? We suspect that the protests would not have spread at all if they had started in a place where uprisings have traditionally been met with violence from the government.

The Arab Spring was a direct tip in that a single action led multiple other actors to act. The directness of this tip might have been facilitated by a contextual tip—the rioters had influence because something had changed within the Middle East. Perhaps that something was technology or social media, which gave the protestors a high degree of connectedness. We leave it to others to determine these effects with greater certainty.[11]

A curious feature of the Arab Spring is not only where it did spread, but also where it did not. Not all Middle Eastern countries joined Tunisia's and Egypt's lead. And, despite some concerns at the time, it did

Figure 4. Top Ten Oil Exporters and Importers

Source: Data from the U.N.; graph from Jones-Rooy 2012b
Dark nodes represent net oil exporters; light nodes represent oil importers.

not spread to other non-democracies, notably China. In theory, a direct tip should involve the whole system—and thus everyone in the world should have eventually joined in protesting against any grievances they might have had. However, in a system, information is not evenly distributed; news about protests in one country does not necessarily spread to another. Jones-Rooy 2012a finds that while the Chinese media mentioned the Arab Spring, they did so cautiously. First, they rarely called it the "Arab Spring"; instead violent clashes in particular countries were mentioned. Second, the media focused on China's reaction to the protests—such as its safe evacuation of Chinese nationals from the region and China's opposition to conflict and to Western involvement. In contrast, the events were portrayed in the United States as connected, promising, and laudable; nicknaming it the "Arab Spring" emphasized its unity as well as its goodness. But even if the Chinese media had portrayed the events in the same way the Western media did, it is unlikely that there would have been a "Chinese Spring" because China already exerts enough control over smaller-scale protests that the flow is stanched before it tips.

It may seem self-evident, but it is worth discussing briefly why the uprisings did not spread to the United States and other Western countries. After all, the Occupy Wall Street movement of late 2011 and early 2012, protests that began in the United States and Canada, did spread to dozens of other countries, such as Australia and Germany. One reason may be that protestors in Tunisia, Egypt, and Libya were operating in similar environments, where a total regime change was more salient than it was to people in the West. Similarly, perhaps, many Chinese citizens (although of course far from all) are thought to be relatively satisfied economically, so it would not have occured to them to see protests in Tunisia as relevant to their lives.

*   *   *

The Arab Spring underscores how advances in complex systems thinking may be applied. Systems thinking allows us to get beyond the "everything matters" trap that one can fall into when thinking about systems. Complexity theorizing can help us unpack which elements in a system matter, how they interact, and to what effect. It is a forecasting as well as a retrospective tool. We are, however, cautious about the powers of prediction that come from using a complexity approach. We may be able to improve our ability to anticipate likely states of the world but we can, at best, only predict probability distributions. But even if they cannot help us with specific predictions, our models can help us to calibrate, explain, compare, and improve our understandings of the world. And, as we showed in the case of the bailout of AIG and not Lehman Brothers, we can use knowledge of system effects to make better policies.

At an even more fundamental level, using complexity theory in social science means adopting a higher tolerance for uncertainty. Systems are by nature messy, intricate, and prone to contingencies, tips, and network changes.[12] The more we appreciate the fact that we are in a system, the more we can build institutions and policies that are robust to a variety of environmental changes. We don't need to know the specific effects of global warming over the next ten years in order to make preparations for it. A basic understanding of the major elements that matter and the range and likelihood of various outcomes, from dire to mild, can suffice to inform policy makers and citizens how they should change their behavior. Deeper knowledge of complex systems and system effects will help us in those endeavors, just as Jervis claimed.

NOTES

1. For another example of systems at work across domains and at a global level, see the description in Zolli and Healy 2012 (1–4) of the causes and consequences of Mexico's food riots in 2007.
2. For an excellent review of the contributions of systems thinking toward climate change see Edwards 2010.
3. See Page 2010 and Mitchell 2009 for surveys of these advances in measuring complexity.
4. Jervis made no claim of originality for either of these observations. The often-curious links between micro-level behaviors and macro-level outcomes, popularized by Schelling, can be traced to Arrow, Nash, and Condorcet. The idea that we cannot consider one domain in isolation goes back to von Forrestor.
5. A related precursor with a focus on informational cascades is Bikhchandani et al. 1992. See Kollman and Page 2005 for a survey of agent-based models in political science.
6. We thank Philip B. K. Potter for this point.
7. For even more details on the role of structure in networks see Jones-Rooy and Page 2010.
8. We don't know whether the government used a related analysis in making its decision. We note only that a consideration of systems effects suggests a set of actions similar to those chosen.

9. It's not as simple as just saying "build this factory here"—although that can happen, too. Often economic or tax incentives in Special Economic Zones in China can be the way the government influences where particular industries end up.
10. It is beyond the scope of this essay to analyze the current system, but many analytical tools, including agent-based modeling and dynamic mathematical techniques, can guide scholars in understanding it. We could conduct a similar analysis in search of evidence of a likely bifurcation in the system, or of a phase transition. Ideally, physicists and international-relations scholars might combine their expertise on this matter.
11. The tip was also a between-class tip as it was a move from a stable equilibrium to a complex one.
12. Page 2008 distinguishes between uncertainty, difficulty, and complexity. Jervis often means a mixture of complexity and uncertainty.

REFERENCES

Arthur, Brian. 1994. *Increasing Returns and Path Dependence in the Economy*. Ann Arbor: University of Michigan Press.
Axelrod, Robert. 1985. *The Evolution of Cooperation*. New York: Basic Books.
Axelrod, Robert. 1997. "The Dissemination of Culture: A Model with Local Convergence and Global Polarization." *The Journal of Conflict Resolution* 41(2): 203–26.
Bak, Per. 1996. *How Nature Works: The Science of Self-Organized Criticality*. New York: Copernicus Press.
Bedau, Mark A. 1997. "Weak Emergence." In *Philosophical Perspectives: Mind, Causation, and World*, vol. 11., Ed. J. Tomberlin. Malden, Mass.: Blackwell.
Bedau, Mark A., and Paul Humphreys, eds. 2008. *Emergence: Contemporary Readings in Philosophy and Science*. Cambridge, Mass.: MIT Press.
Bednar, Jenna, Aaron Bramson, Andrea Jones-Rooy, and Scott E. Page. 2010. "Emergent Cultural Signatures and Persistent Diversity: A Model of Conformity and Consistency." *Rationality and Society* 19(1): 65–97.
Bhavnani, Ravi. 2003. "Adaptive Agents, Political Institutions, and Civic Traditions in Modern Italy." *Journal of Artificial Societies and Social Simulation* 6(4). http://jasss.soc.surrey.ac.uk/6/4/1.html.
Bikhchandani, Sushil, David Hirshleifer, and Ivo Welch. 1992. "A Theory of Fads, Fashion, Custom, and Cultural Change as Informational Cascades." *Journal of Political Economy* 100(5): 992–1026.
Callaway, D. S., M.E.J. Newman, S. H. Strogatz, and D. J. Watts. 2000. "Network Robustness and Fragility: Percolation on Random Graphs." *Physical Review Letters* 85: 5468–71.
Casey, Michael. 2012. *The Unfair Trade: How Our Broken Global Financial System Destroys the Middle Class*. New York: Crown Business.
Cederman, Lars-Erik. 1997. *Emergent Actors in World Politics*. Princeton: Princeton University Press.

Clarke, Kevin A., and David M. Primo. 2012. *A Model Discipline: Political Science and the Logic of Representations*. New York: Oxford University Press.

David, Paul A. 1994. "Why Are Institutions the 'Carriers of History'?: Path Dependence and the Evolution of Conventions, Organizations, and Institutions." *Structural Change and Economic Dynamics* 5(2): 205–20.

David, Paul A. 2007. "Path Dependence: A Foundational Concept for Historical Social Science." *Cliometrica—The Journal of Historical Economics and Econometric History* 1(2): 1–25.

de Marchi, Scott. 2005. *Computational and Mathematical Modeling in the Social Sciences*. Cambridge: Cambridge University Press.

Edwards, Paul N. 2010. *A Vast Machine: Computer Models, Climate Data, and the Politics of Global Warming*. Cambridge, Mass.: MIT Press.

Epstein, Josh. 2006. *Generative Social Science: Studies in Agent-Based Computational Modeling*. Princeton: Princeton University Press.

Christakis, Nicholas A., and James H. Fowler. 2009. *Connected: The Surprising Power of Our Social Networks and How They Shape Our Lives: How Your Friends' Friends Affect Everything You Feel, Think, and Do*. New York: Little, Brown, and Company.

Hausmann, Ricardo, and Cesar Hidalgo. 2009. "The Building Blocks of Economic Complexity." *Proceedings of the National Academy of Sciences* 106(26): 10570–75.

Holland, John. 1998. *Emergence: From Chaos to Order*. New York: Perseus Books.

IMF (International Monetary Fund). 2009. "World Global Financial Stability Report." April. Washington, D.C.: International Monetary Fund.

Jackson, J. E., and Ken Kollman. 2010. "A Formulation of Path Dependence with an Empirical Example." *Quarterly Journal of Political Science* 5(3): 257–89.

Jervis, Robert. 1997. *System Effects: Complexity in Political and Social Life*. Princeton: Princeton University Press.

Jones-Rooy, Andrea E. 2012a. *Communication and Commitment: The Strategic Use of the Media in China and Other Autocracies*. University of Michigan, political science, Ph.D. diss.

Jones-Rooy, Andrea E. 2012b. "Network Stability of China's Oil Transactions." University of Michigan, working paper.

Jones-Rooy, Andrea, and Scott E. Page. 2010. "The Complexities of Global Systems History." *The Journal of the Historical Society* 10(3): 345–65.

Joyce, Kyle A. 2012. "The Cascading Dynamics of War Expansion." University of California, Davis, working paper.

Kalyvas, Stathis. 1999. "The Decay and Breakdown of Communist One-Party Systems." *Annual Review of Political Science* 2: 323–43.

King, Gary, Jennifer Pan, and Molly Roberts. 2012. "How Censorship in China Allows Government Criticism but Silences Collective Expression." Manuscript.

Kollman, Ken, and Scott Page. 2005. "Computational Political Economy." In *The Handbook of Computational Economics*, ed. Leigh Tesfatsion and Kenneth Judd. North Holland: Elsevier.

Kollman, Ken. 2012. "The Potential Value of Computational Models in Social Science Research." In *Oxford Handbook in Philosophy in the Social Sciences*, ed. Harold Kincaid. New York: Oxford University Press.

Lamberson, P. J., and Scott E. Page. 2012. "Tipping Points." *Quarterly Journal of Political Science* 7: 175–208.

Laver, Michael. 2005. "Policy and the Dynamics of Political Competition." *American Political Science Review* 99(2): 263–81.

Laver, M. 2007. "Agent-based Models of Party Competition: Analysis and/or Exploration?" Presented at the American Political Science Association annual meeting.

Lustick, Ian, and Dan Miodownik. 2000. "Deliberative Democracy and Public Discourse: The Agent-Based Argument Repertoire Model." *Complexity* 5(4): 13–30.

Maoz, Zev. 2010. *Networks of Nations: The Evolution, Structure, and Impact of International Networks, 1816–2001*. Cambridge: Cambridge University Press.

Miller, John, and Scott E. Page. 2007. *Complex Adaptive Systems: Computational Models of Social Life*. Princeton: Princeton University Press.

Mitchell, Melanie. 2009. *Complexity: A Guided Tour*. Oxford: Oxford University Press.

Page, Scott E. 2006. "Path Dependence." *Quarterly Journal of Political Science* 1(1): 87–115.

Page, Scott E. 2007. *The Difference: How the Power of Diversity Creates Better Groups, Teams, Schools, and Societies*. Princeton: Princeton University Press.

Page, Scott E. 2008. "Uncertainty, Difficulty, and Complexity." *Journal of Theoretical Politics* 20: 115–49.

Page, Scott E. 2010. *Diversity and Complexity*. Princeton: Princeton University Press.

Pierson, Paul. 2000. "Increasing Returns, Path Dependence, and the Study of Politics." *American Political Science Review* 94(2): 251–67.

Pierson, Paul. 2004. *Politics in Time: History, Institutions, and Social Analysis*. Princeton: Princeton University Press.

Potter, Philip B. K. 2012. "Terrorism and Two Chinas." University of Michigan working paper.

Sang-Hun, Choe. 2012. "North Korea Experts Can See a Lot in a Hemline." *New York Times* July 15.

Shipan, Charles R., and Craig Volden. 2008. "The Mechanisms of Policy Diffusion." *American Journal of Political Science* 52(4): 840–57.

Solé, Ricard V. 2011. *Phase Transitions*. Princeton: Princeton University Press.

Sterman, J. D. 2000. *Business Systems Dynamics: Systems Thinking and Modeling for a Complex Word*. New York: McGraw-Hill.

Watts, Duncan. 2011. *Everything Is Obvious: Once You Know the Answer*. New York: Crown Books.

Wolfram, Stephen. 2002. *A New Kind of Science*. Champaign, Ill.: Wolfram Media.

Zolli, Andrew, and Ann Marie Healy. 2012. *Resilience: Why Things Bounce Back*. New York: Free Press.

Nuno P. Monteiro

WE CAN NEVER STUDY MERELY ONE THING: REFLECTIONS ON SYSTEMS THINKING AND IR

ABSTRACT: *Robert Jervis's* System Effects *was published just as systems thinking began to decline among political scientists, who were adopting increasingly strict standards of causal identification, privileging experimental and large-N studies. Many politically consequential system effects are not amenable to research designs that meet these standards, yet they must nonetheless be studied if the most important questions of international politics are to be answered. For example, if nuclear weapons are considered in light of their effect on the international system as a whole, it becomes clear that they have obviated the need for a global balance of power by allowing states to counterbalance threats by acquiring nuclear weapons rather than investing in massive conventional balancing efforts. Similarly, systems thinking should inform our understanding of the impact of a "unipolar power" such as the United States, which has enjoyed an overwhelming preponderance of conventional military power since the fall of the Berlin Wall. A unipolar power is likely to become involved in frequent conflicts because it is not restrained by the presence of a peer competitor.*

The aphoristic version of Robert Jervis's *System Effects: Complexity in Political and Social Life* (Princeton University Press, 1997) is that "we can never do merely one thing."[1] Any action in a system will have multiple, intertwining effects. If this is so, we can never study merely one thing either. What does this mean for scholars of international relations, who study one of the most complex social systems of all, global politics?

Nuno P. Monteiro, Department of Political Science, Yale University, has published in *International Organization*, *International Security*, and *International Theory*.

Without attempting to settle such a broad question in such a short piece, I will use this article to explore several of its aspects. I start by laying out the core of Jervis's view on systems and their effects for international politics. Then, I trace the causes and consequences of the decline of systems thinking in the field of International Relations (IR)[2] since the publication of Jervis's book and reflect on its future application. Finally, I exemplify the implications of Jervis's views by applying them to two particularly important issues in contemporary international politics: nuclear weapons and U.S. power preponderance.

What Is a System?

According to Jervis (1997, 6), "we are dealing with a system when (a) a set of units or elements is interconnected so that changes in some elements or their relations produce changes in other parts of the system, and (b) the entire system exhibits properties and behaviors that are different from those of the parts." A system's key properties are, therefore, interconnectedness and non-additivity. Together, these two features of a system manifest themselves through what Jervis calls "system effects," with consequences for both those acting within a system and those studying it. Specifically, system effects limit both the control that political decision makers exercise over the outcomes of their actions and the explanatory power of the theories that scholars develop to explain those outcomes. The bulk of Jervis's book is thus devoted to highlighting the ways in which system effects complicate the consequences of decision makers' actions—and scholars' attempts to establish their causes.

Overall, Jervis finds at least four types of system effects. Each of them is the focus of a particular line of IR research.

The first relates to how one actor's preferences and strategies affect those of others. In IR, this type of system effect has been the object of abundant scholarship, using both formal and informal game-theoretic tools to study dynamics such as the security dilemma (Jervis 1978), coercion and escalation (Schelling 1960 and 1966), and the causes of war (Fearon 1995; Powell 2006).

The second type of system effect analyzed by Jervis centers on the complications produced by the interaction of more than two players. This has been the object of two types of IR scholarship. Some scholars have used multiplayer game theory to study, for example, the dynamics of hegemonic stability (Snidal 1985) or international alliances (Morrow 1994). Other scholars have used computer simulations and complex adaptive systems to explore the evolution of the international system (Pepinsky 2005).

Third, Jervis discusses the constraints imposed on actors by the structure of the system in which they operate. This type of system effect is well known to those familiar with systemic theorizing in IR, as it is the focus of structural realism (Waltz 1979; Mearsheimer 2001; Glaser 2010), the most self-consciously systemic brand of IR scholarship.

Finally, Jervis looks at the reverse system effect: how actors affect the structure of the system they populate. This dynamic informs much social theory (Giddens 1984) and in IR it is the object of process theory, a subfield of recent constructivist scholarship (Wendt 1999; Jackson and Nexon 1999; Pouliot 2008).

Why Social Systems Are Hard to Predict

Although these effects are produced by any type of system, according to Jervis they are particularly important in social systems. Unlike the agents that populate natural systems, social actors are reflective and can therefore change their preferences and strategies as a result of interactions with other agents, changes in structural conditions, and even their knowledge of particular theories about the consequences of their behavior. The self-reflective character of the actors that populate the international system—states, political leaders, international organizations, and so on—therefore limits the predictive power of both those acting within the system and of those observing it, complicating the status of IR theories.

Take, for instance, the case of domino theory, which Jervis (165–76, 266–69) discusses at length. Because of system effects, domino theory's central prediction—that an agent's display of weakness on one particular issue will create a reputation for weakness that will, in turn, lead other agents to push aggressively on other issues, leading to a string of negative outcomes following the initial concession—is difficult to test. If political leaders believe this prediction, then after making a concession they will take actions that boost the credibility of their other commitments. These actions will have the effect of preventing the dominos from falling. Jervis calls this the "domino theory paradox": political actors' belief in domino theory leads them to implement policies that ultimately falsify it.

What, then, is the truth-status of domino theory? Its empirical falsification seems to depend on political leaders believing it to be true. If, on the contrary, its truth were not taken for granted, it might well be true.

Similarly, let's postulate for a moment that political leaders believe that the theory of offensive realism (Mearsheimer 2001) is correct. Drawing on historical evidence, this theory claims that political leaders consistently try to maximize the relative power of their states in an attempt to become a global hegemon. At the same time, because of system effects such as counterbalancing or the limitations to power projection created by oceans, offensive realists show that past political leaders have consistently been defeated in their hegemonic ambitions. Believing this, future political leaders might no longer attempt to turn their state into a global hegemon, thereby falsifying the theory at least in its prescriptive dimension.

How can we theorize in such circumstances?

In *System Effects*, Jervis aims at helping us develop the intellectual apparatus necessary to deal with such predicaments, with a particular emphasis on international politics. Philosophically, the purpose of his book is to combat our *anosognosia* (our lack of awareness about our ignorance) of system effects. Jervis reveals the system effects that shape and shove international politics, turning them from "unknown unknowns" into "known unknowns" to better inform our decision making and theorizing. The point is not to wish away the complexity of systems, rather to make actors and policy makers aware of it.

The Decline of Systems Thinking in IR

Systems thinking has been a perennial element of IR theory. Concepts such as relative power—reflecting the view that the expected consequences of one's actions must take into account the expected reactions of others—have been invoked at least since Thucydides used it to explain the origins of the Peloponnesian War. Likewise, the balance of power—perhaps the oldest, most pervasive concept in IR theory (Little 2007)—reflects a systems approach to thinking about international politics: Whatever one state does to disrupt the balance and gain a preponderance of power, other states will thwart that goal, re-establishing an equilibrium among them (Nexon 2009). Yet despite Jervis's encouragement to think in more sophisticated systems terms about international politics, systems thinking has been on the wane in IR during the fifteen years since the publication of his book.

To put this development in historical context—and painting with a very broad brush—between the mid-1960s and the late 1970s, IR was dominated by empiricist, inductive approaches (Russett 1969; Schmidt 2002). This type of scholarship aimed at establishing some ground truths by amassing facts about international politics that had until then eluded any systematic, objective treatment. Then Kenneth Waltz published his *Theory of International Politics* in 1979, explicitly trying to carve out a space for theory—systems theory, in fact. Waltz was so successful in this aim that the almost two decades between the publication of his book and Jervis's *System Effects* were a period during which IR was consumed with theoretical, often paradigmatic, disputes, with neorealism, neoliberalism, and later constructivism vying for primacy as *the* right lens through which to understand international politics (Keohane 1986; Hollis and Smith 1990; Monteiro and Ruby 2009). In sum, for twenty years after the publication of Waltz's book, grand systemic theorizing reigned supreme in IR.

Inevitably, this situation produced a backlash. Around the time *System Effects* came out, the pendulum started to swing back towards more empirical research and, at most, some mid-level theorizing. Since the late 1990s, systems theory, formal game-theoretic models, constructivist process theory, and computer simulations have all either declined or failed to live up to their initial promise. In my view, this decline is the result of mutually interacting intellectual and professional changes flowing from the rise of increasingly strict standards for identifying causal relationships, a trend that emerged throughout political science more generally.

The "question of causal identification" is the question of how we know that cause x has produced effect y. For positivists, who dominate the mainstream of U.S. political science, knowledge is at its most scientific when we can establish causation cleanly—i.e., when we can be certain that what we call the cause has indeed caused the effect, without the intervening action of other variables. The gold standard for producing this kind of knowledge is the experimental method. Our causal inferences are stronger when based on experiments in which the posited cause can be turned into a "treatment" and applied to subjects that are chosen randomly or "as-if" randomly from a representative sample of the population, while the remaining subjects in the sample are presented with a control situation that is identical save for the absence of the treatment.

Such data can be generated by conducting laboratory (Webster and Sell 2007) or field experiments (Gerber and Green 2012), or by leveraging natural experiments (Dunning 2012). Second best to experimental data is large-N observational data, which may suffer from manifold biases but nonetheless (in the eyes of most social scientists) produces robust, statistically significant correlations on which we can pin our causal beliefs. At the bottom of the causal-identification totem pole are research designs that focus on relatively rare phenomena and rely on qualitative evidence to study them.

Alas, the types of questions that would benefit from systems thinking tend not to be susceptible to experimental or large-N quantitative answers, for two reasons.

First, the types of questions for which systems thinking is more important and fruitful, and indeed the questions for which systems thinking has been used in the study of international relations, tend to render experimental methodologies unfeasible, unethical, or impractical. For example, our ability to conduct experimental research on the origins of major wars, the sources of systemic change in international politics, the causes of nuclear proliferation, or the dynamics of nuclear escalation is quite limited. Furthermore, data on these questions is also limited, making large-N observational studies (deemed second best to an experimental research design) often also unfeasible. Our ability to study these questions using the two most reliable methods of causal identification is therefore restricted.[3]

Second, the nature of system effects undermines the advantages of stricter identification standards, such as the experimental method. The rules of the experimental method—according to which the only thing that can vary between control and treatment groups is the treatment—are incompatible with Jervis's contention that, in a system, we cannot do merely one thing. If we want to capture system effects, then, the experimental setting is not our best friend. Of course, we can use experiments to attempt to isolate particular system effects. But in studying the interaction of multiple system effects, experimental methods, even when usable, would have little if any advantage over other, supposedly weaker, causal-identification strategies. By trying to change merely one thing (the treatment) at a time, scientists create an "unsystemic" environment from which system effects are artificially absent.

One could take this to mean that scientific methods cannot deal with the problems generated by system effects and that, consequently, we cannot have a science of IR—or a social science, for that matter, since societies and economies, not just international relations, are systems and therefore experience system effects.

I think this interpretation of the situation goes too far, because it is premised on an arbitrarily restrictive view of science for which we have no justification (Monteiro and Ruby 2009). Whether science (regardless of the methods it uses) can get at the way the world *really* works is not only an unsettled question, it is an unanswerable one. Our inability to ground science on a firm foundational footing—or to prove conclusively that such ground does not exist—should lead us to endorse a sort of foundational prudence, so we can continue to muddle through with our attempts to gain knowledge on different questions using the theoretical and methodological stances most adequate to each.

In addition, there is much to be learned about the workings of international politics in the area that lies between, on the one hand, the strictures of the experimental method and, on the other, the intractability of trying to capture all possible system effects produced by a particular policy or action. In this wide middle ground, we can continue with our attempts to illuminate how taking action x—despite the myriad unpredicted consequences it may have, as a result of system effects—is, on average, more likely than not to produce consequence y.

Jervis's work should therefore not be read as an invitation to abandon the scientific study of systems. Rather, it is an invitation to acknowledge the complications that system effects introduce in research on phenomena that take place in a systemic setting, and to adapt our methodological expectations accordingly.

Nevertheless, the rise in the standards for identification of causal power that we have witnessed in political science over the last two decades has led many IR scholars to abandon approaches that have a systems dimension to them. Instead, they have pursued more clear-cut research designs and have asked questions that are more amenable to being answered by such designs. As a result, many of the most important questions of international politics receive less scholarly attention than they did two decades ago, as do theoretical approaches such as systems theory. In turn, conducting research on systems questions reduces one's ability to publish in top peer-reviewed journals, gain professional promotion at top research universities, and, more generally, win scholarly recognition. Furthermore, faculty members want to train graduate students—and graduate students want to be trained—in the approaches that maximize their chances of producing research that is considered to be on the cutting edge. Increasingly, such research is defined in terms of its design rather than its question, in what is currently called "design-based research" (Dunning 2012). Thus, the shift in intellectual standards has been reinforced in exactly the manner that Jervis might have predicted for the "system" consisting of international-relations scholars. This has all but precluded political scientists from asking the types of questions about international affairs for which systems thinking can be more useful.

Now, I think most scholars—at least most positivists (and I think Jervis is a soft positivist)—would agree that we should use the highest standard of causal identification available for any given research question. But as a profession, IR faces a difficult choice: it can uphold the latest, most stringent standard of causal identification, using it as a research design yardstick which then restricts the domain of questions that members of the discipline can study; or it can relax identification standards to allow for research on issues that are not always amenable to being studied using the highest causal identification standards.

A more calibrated approach to the problem of causal identification would keep identification standards in a dialogue with the political importance of each particular question. If a research question is politically important—i.e., if it has the potential to affect the lives of numerous people in important ways—we should not abstain from studying it, regardless of whether it is amenable to the most demanding criteria of causal identification. Instead, we should study it by using the best research design to which it *is* amenable.[4]

The litmus test a particular causal identification standard has to pass in order to deserve broad application is whether we would live in a better world were we to "forget" all the research done using designs that are less reliable at causal identification.[5] A quick thought experiment may prove instructive on this point. Would we be better off without our vast array of scholarship on nuclear deterrence—a field built upon scant empirical data, because nuclear crises are relatively rare and nuclear exchanges have never taken place? Likewise, would we be better off without any knowledge of deterrence merely because the questions associated with it—how to modulate escalation, how to bargain under the shadow of terror, how to convert arms to influence, etc.—are made so complex by the system effects at play in crisis dynamics that we cannot come up with experimental or large-N research designs to study them? I think not. What we need is a healthier dialogue between identification standards and complex but important political questions.

The Future of Systems Thinking in IR

For the most part, IR scholars associate systems thinking with systemic theories and, in particular, with structural neorealism (Waltz 1979; Mearsheimer 2001; Glaser 2010). But this need not be the case. The different system effects highlighted by Jervis can be studied only by using different approaches, of which structural neorealism, like systemic theorizing more broadly, is only one important instance.

The first step to encourage further use of systems thinking in IR is to separate it from a particular style of work, systemic theorizing, that is only one of several ways of thinking about system effects. In other words, we need to separate *system* effects from *systemic* effects. System effects take place within any system, even one with just two actors and a very simple structure, e.g., two-player games such as the stag hunt, prisoners' dilemma, or chicken (Schelling 1966; Jervis 1978). Systemic or structural theories are designed to capture this type of system effect when it applies to the entire international system: how its structure imposes constraints on the states that populate it. But the entire international system is made up of numerous sub-systems, down to the smallest ones, all of which generate their own system effects. So there are plenty of applications of systems thinking beyond structural theory. In short, many system effects are not systemic.

A second step towards greater use of systems thinking in IR would be to emphasize the possibility of incorporating it without discarding all hope of establishing causal effects. At the limit, a systems approach in which nothing is taken for granted—in which no *ceteris paribus* analyses are acceptable, and all the types of system effects described by Jervis are at work all the time, with strong consequences—would all but negate causality. As Jervis (1997, 57–58) puts it, "as actions combine to constitute the environment in which the actors are situated and actors in turn change as the environment alters, the language of dependent and independent variables becomes problematic."

This need not be the case, however. Systems thinking can take many forms, depending upon the constraints we impose on what is endogenous and what is exogenous to the theory. In fact, at least with the conceptual tools we have available today, we will not get any purchase on system effects unless we ignore or fix the complications introduced by some of them in order to study others. For instance, it will be difficult to study the effects of indirect interactions among three states if we do not bracket the issue of how these will transform the environment in which they interact. Conversely, in order to study how actors transform the environment in which they exist, we will likely have to abstain, at least in part, from understanding other system effects. Even strong constructivists who focus on questions of "mutual constitution"—questions that cannot be settled by looking at causal relationships, because the two variables affect each other—agree on fixing or abstracting from some parts of the world in order to interpret others.

Put differently, we need to allow for the study of system effects to vary according to two dimensions: the scope of the system we analyze and the scope of the variables we endogenize. This creates the typology of systems thinking presented in Table 1.

Although typologies require strong simplifications, I want to use this one to make two points.

First, systems thinking can be incorporated in small doses by studying particular system effects without endogenizing everything. For instance, two-player game-theoretic models have significant purchase over many

Table 1. Typology of Systems Thinking in IR

		scope of system	
		small	large
scope of endogenization	small	two-player game-theory	structural realism, multi-player game-theory
	large	constructivism	structural constructivism, process theory, computer simulations

of the system effects that relate to how one actor's preferences and strategies affect those of others. The fact that it can do so without endogenizing many other processes (such as, for instance, the effect of actors on their environment) may very well be what makes it relatively easy for two-player game theory to generate testable empirical implications (although it does so less than it should). Similarly, structural IR theories focus on a particular type of system effect—systemic constraints—without allowing others, such as two-player dynamic interactions à la game-theoretic models, to factor in.[6]

Second, the different types of systems work listed in the table are in a complementary relationship with each other, not a competitive one, because they are not trying to explain the same system effects. Thus, process theory studies the sequences through which agents such as states reshape the structure of international politics—for instance, by gradually introducing international law as a constraint on state action (Koskenniemi 2001). Studying that process requires focusing on the bottom-up actions of various states that, over a long period of time, ended up producing the structural constraint that we to refer as international law. This is compatible with using a top-down, structural approach to studying the system effects of this new structure on the behavior of states. Similarly, constructivist scholarship devotes a great deal of attention to the processes through which norms emerge, spread, and become ingrained (Finnemore and Sikkink 1998). This is compatible with the subsequent use of two-player game-theoretic models in which the willingness to abide by certain norms is incorporated into the preference functions of the actors.

Much of the future added value of systems thinking in IR may come from the intersection of these different types of work. To make the point with a broad example: Structural realists generally argue that relative power, measured by material factors, is an important variable in determining how states will behave and thus, ultimately, in establishing systemic peace and stability. In structural-realist work, ideology is (with the puzzling exception of nationalism) merely a tool used by statesmen to advance their goals of security or power maximization. Structural constructivist scholarship, on the other hand, focuses on the role of ideology and norms in shaping the ways states interact in a systemic culture that, in turn, determines their needs for different levels and types of material capabilities, depending on the level of enmity and threat in the system (Wendt 1999). But whence do these norms come? To answer that question, we must resort to process theory, which focuses on the production of normative content by agents and its spread through social systems. How, then, do material capabilities foster the spread of norms by determining the power of different actors that participate in the process of spreading them? Only by paying attention to the ideational processes that change the structure of the international system *in a particular material context* will we be able to get a handle on this question (Barkin 2010).

In sum, in order fully to incorporate the power of system effects in theories of international politics, we need to embrace a political epistemology that captures the multiple factors that go into the process through which each agent forms its political views, and this, in turn, requires that we incorporate the interaction of material and ideational factors.

Let me now flesh out these ideas in two areas where system effects play an important role: nuclear weapons and U.S. power preponderance.

Nuclear Weapons and Systems Thinking

The introduction of nuclear weapons was significant enough to deserve the epithet of a "nuclear revolution" (Jervis 1989). Still, most academic work on nuclear weapons treats them as a unit-level variable. Seen from this perspective, they have consequences primarily for those states that possess them, and for those engaged in disputes with nuclear states.

Jervis's book invites us to think about nuclear weapons as a systemic variable, however. In other words, we should reflect on the role of nuclear weapons as a technology that transforms the structure of the international system in ways that go beyond the direct effects of nuclear possession by particular states.

In what follows, I focus on the effects of the nuclear revolution for balance-of-power theory. Specifically, I explore the impact of the nuclear revolution on the relationship between balancing, which is a state strategy, and the systemic balance of power, which is a systemic outcome. I contend that the nuclear revolution makes it possible for states successfully to achieve the goal of balancing (i.e., guaranteeing their survival) without producing a systemic balance of power.

Balance-of-power theory is usually presented as having a natural-law-like quality: states' need to ensure their own survival against a background of systemic anarchy inevitably leads to a particular outcome—a systemic balance of power (Nexon 2009). As is often the case with the "naturalization" of social laws, the contingency inherent in the relationship between balancing mechanisms and systemic balances of power is hidden by this understanding of power balances as inevitable. Jervis's work on system effects allows us to question the taken-for-granted nature of the relationship between balancing and systemic balances of power in the shadow of the nuclear revolution.

The core logic of any balance-of-power theory is relatively straightforward. States care first and foremost about their own survival. An unmatched concentration of power in one state threatens the survival of the others. In order to improve their odds of survival, the others will therefore balance against concentrated power. Threats to survival are minimized only by amassing at least as much power as is possessed by any other state. Balancing efforts will therefore lead to the emergence of a systemic balance of power.

I do not wish to question the notion that survival is the first goal of states. But in the nuclear age, the remaining steps in the balance-of-power logic do not necessarily follow, because now an unmatched concentration of power in one state does not necessarily threaten the survival of others. Therefore, states' attempts to improve their odds of survival by balancing against concentrated power do not necessarily lead them to amass as much power as any other state; that much power may not be necessary to minimize threats to state survival. Thus, balancing efforts—even successful ones—may not produce a systemic balance of power.

An unmatched concentration of power in one state threatens the survival of others only if survival depends on a balance of power. This is the case in a conventionally armed world, where a state needs to possess roughly matching forces to deter a competitor's attack. Conventional inferiority vis-à-vis another state leads to military vulnerability and the inability to deter the adversary, ultimately undermining state survival.

In contrast, deterrence between powers with survivable nuclear arsenals is based on each state being unable to avoid suffering horrendous costs at the hands of the other in the case of an all-out conflict. Since this ability does not depend on a balance of conventional power, the possibility that a small nuclear arsenal can inflict a devastating retaliatory strike may deter any state—even one significantly more powerful in nuclear or conventional terms—from threatening the survival of the less powerful state. Therefore, states that acquire a nuclear arsenal have virtually guaranteed their survival even though they may possess negligible conventional capabilities. In a nuclear world, the connection between threat minimization and a systemic balance of power is severed. This possibility requires us to revise the view that a given state is able to guarantee its survival, and therefore stop its balancing efforts, only once it has amassed as much power as any other state (Monteiro 2009; Deudney 2011).

In a nuclear world, in fact, the pursuit of an overall (i.e., nuclear and conventional) balance of power between nuclear states is futile at best and dangerous at worst for a state's survival. Since two nuclear states are unlikely to go to war with each other—and, in any case, such a war would threaten the survival of both, regardless of the conventional balance of power between them—conventional balancing efforts between them for the purpose of assuring state survival would be relatively futile. Conventional balancing efforts could even be dangerous because an attempt to acquire conventional forces capable of being used against other nuclear states could be perceived by the latter as indicative of aggressive intentions, triggering preventive action (Debs and Monteiro 2012).

Furthermore, as Jervis (1997, 122) points out, nuclear weapons, by guaranteeing state survival, make alliances less important. It is senseless for several states to pool their nuclear or conventional resources to counteract a state that could destroy them anyway. This line of reasoning highlights the theoretical contradiction underlying mechanistic understandings of the formation of systemic balances of power.

As Jervis (1997, 132) writes, for a systemic balance of power to emerge, "war must be a viable tool of statecraft." The reasoning goes like this: States care about their survival; therefore, they must be able credibly to threaten potential adversaries with high costs in case of a major war; and the only way of doing so is to balance until they possess as much as or more power than any such potentially predatory state. Nuclear weapons, however, raise the costs of war to the point at which it no longer is a viable tool of statecraft among the most powerful states in the system. In fact, nuclear weapons make all-out great-power war unwinnable (Jervis 1989). This means that a major war in a nuclear world endangers a state's existence, jeopardizing the initial premise of the argument that led to balancing in the first place: states' preeminent interest in their own survival. Consequently, any threat of major war issued by a nuclear state against another nuclear state threatens the survival of the state that issues it. In sum, nuclear weapons make the *ultima ratio* of international politics—the ability to wage major war rather than allow an adversary to threaten a state's existence—absurd. It would be, in Bismarck's words, suicide for fear of death.

Conversely, Jervis has argued, invulnerable nuclear arsenals make it very difficult to prevent *any* war between great powers from escalating into a total nuclear war. As he explains, all-out war is the result of "a dynamic process in which both sides get more and more deeply involved, more and more expectant, more and more concerned not to be a slow second in case the war starts" (Jervis 1989, 19). For a nuclear war to remain limited, and therefore winnable, one of the belligerents must be willing to give up while retaining the capability to inflict devastating damage on the other side (Craig 2003, 30). To the extent that defeat would risk state survival, this violates the first premise of balance-of-power theory: that states care first and foremost about their own survival.

Nuclear weapons therefore give paramount practical import to the distinction between theories of balancing and balance-of-power theories. As Daniel Nexon has pointed out, the extant literature often conflates the two, despite their lack of logical coherence. But theories that explain the conditions behind a strategy of balancing and the ways of implementing it (i.e., theories of balancing) are logically independent from theories that explain the formation of balance of power at the systemic level (i.e., balance-of-power theories). In Nexon's (2009, 340) words, "even theories that posit the ubiquity of balancing strategies need not imply that these strategies aggregate into systemic power balances." Balancing may be a common state strategy, yet the international system as a whole might be persistently out of balance. Nuclear weapons bring this disjunction into bold relief.

This leads us to the next topic to which I want to apply systems thinking: U.S. power preponderance.

Unipolarity and Systems Thinking

Since the collapse of the Soviet Union in 1989–91, the United States has enjoyed a position unique among that of modern states: it possesses far more military power-projection capabilities than any of its peers. As we saw in the previous section, nuclear weapons make this situation potentially durable. In a nuclear world, to use Jervis's (1997, 275) terminology, an international system with a preponderant power can reach a condition of quasi-homeostasis. In this section, I use systems thinking to highlight four other key features of the current era of U.S. power preponderance.

First, in order to explain why the overwhelming military power at Washington's disposal is "allowed" by other states, we must combine the effect of nuclear weapons on the need for balancing strategies, mentioned above, with two other factors.

The first is the historical trajectory through which power preponderance emerged. The United States happened upon its current position as a result of the Soviet collapse. Granted, Washington devoted massive resources to building up a first-rate military throughout the Cold War. But it did so in order to compete with another great power, the Soviet Union, which threatened the stability—some would say the viability—of the Western way of life. But the movement from being one of two great powers to becoming the uncontested foremost power in global military affairs was not the result of an intentional process. The United States did not gradually become *primus inter pares*. Rather, it acquired that position by the sudden disintegration of its only competitor.

In systems-thinking terms, this highlights the role of hysteresis, the fact that the "status of a system at a particular point . . . depends not only on the state of particular variables, but also on how that state was reached" (Jervis 1997, 38). Had the current U.S. power preponderance been the result of an intentional effort on the part of the United States to obtain it, it is likely that other states, suspicious of U.S. motives, would have stymied it early on through counterbalancing. Because aiming explicitly at global power preponderance signals aggressive intent, even nuclear states would have been likely to balance against a state keen on attaining it. In sum, the radical transformation of the international system produced by the Soviet collapse made possible the relatively stable nature of the post-Cold War system.

Second, system effects are useful to understand how U.S. power preponderance has a nuanced effect on war-producing mechanisms. On the one hand, power preponderance dampens the odds of competition and conflict among major powers (Wohlforth 1999). On the other hand, however, recent scholarship has highlighted the ways in which power preponderance also fosters conflict (Monteiro 2011/12).

The basic intuition behind this last argument is based on the type of indirect effects emphasized by systems thinking. When the world is organized into two or more blocs, each headed by a great power, weaker states can typically find an ally to boost their odds of survival in the face of a threat. So, for instance, if the United States or one of its allies threatened a weaker country during the Cold War, that country would be likely to seek and obtain Soviet support and sponsorship. In a world with a preponderant power, however, a state that feels threatened by it has no potential great-power sponsor.

This imbalance, by lowering the costs of war between a preponderant power such as the United States and a relatively weak state, has two concurrent effects. First, it boosts the bargaining leverage enjoyed by the United States in disputes with weak states unless its demands are so problematic (either because of their magnitude or the possibility that they will be recurrent) that the weak state has an incentive to resist them, risking war (Sechser 2010). Second, it weakens the credibility of U.S. negative assurances, undermining the coercive capability of U.S. pronouncements. Coercion requires both a credible threat of punishment being meted out in case the target ignores the coercive demands, and a credible assurance of punishment being withheld in case the target complies with them. A situation of power preponderance such as the one the United States enjoys today boosts the former but weakens the latter, making coercive attempts more likely to break down in war (Monteiro 2009). In sum, the indirect effects of its power preponderance help explain why the United States has been at war for fourteen out of the twenty three years since the Soviet Union abdicated its great-power status in 1989.

Third, system effects can help us understand why, despite conditions under which nuclear proliferation was expected to be rampant, we have seen very few attempts to acquire nuclear weapons since the end of the Cold War. Writing about the consequences of widespread nuclear proliferation, Jervis (2009, 213) worried that unipolarity may "have within it the seeds if not of its own destruction, then at least of its modification." As we saw in the previous section, nuclear weapons virtually guarantee the survival of any state—even a conventionally weak state faced with a global hegemon such as the United States. This should result in nuclear proliferation, as more states opt for acquiring the ultimate deterrent in order to ensure their survival. Still, only a handful of states have maintained nuclear programs with military goals since the end of the Cold War. Two have abandoned their nuclear ambitions: Iraq in 1995 and Libya in 2003. Two more are suspected of having ongoing nuclear programs: Iran and Syria. Perhaps more importantly, only one state managed to acquire nuclear weapons since the collapse of the Soviet Union: North Korea in 2006.

What explains this limited rate of proliferation, with only one new nuclear power in the past two decades, is the indirect effect of U.S. power preponderance. States that would value nuclear weapons know that they may be the target of a preventive strike by the United States aimed at avoiding proliferation. The lower the cost of an effective preventive strike, the more likely it is to happen. Therefore, U.S. power preponderance, by lowering the costs of counter-proliferation preventive strikes and making them potentially more effective, reduces the odds that a state willing to develop nuclear weapons will indeed get the opportunity to do so. Only by studying the interaction between the preferences (and strategies) of states considering nuclear acquisition with those of the United States can we explain the low rate of proliferation after the end of the Cold War (Monteiro and Debs 2012). In this instance, military power preponderance was self-sustaining.

Finally, system effects are crucial in evaluating the value of global power preponderance. What benefits does a state extract from it? What can it do that it could not were there to be a peer competitor?

It is possible that—at least in the security realm—power preponderance does not come with greater influence over international outcomes (Glaser 2011). As we saw in the previous section, in a nuclear world, power preponderance does not add much in terms of ensuring state survival. If states can ensure their survival short of establishing a systemic balance of power, then, *a fortiori*, they do not need to enjoy a preponderance of power to secure it. Likewise, power preponderance does not add much to a state's ability to project a security umbrella over its allies. In other words, preponderance is not necessary to provide credible extended deterrence guarantees to other states. After all, the United States was able to deter a Soviet invasion of Western Europe throughout the Cold War.

The only circumstances in which a preponderance of power may present a benefit in this respect would be in the case of a potential competitor assuming an extremely aggressive, risk-seeking posture (Glaser 2011, 141). Such a posture, however, would be self-defeating in a nuclear world, and is therefore highly unlikely. Absent extremely revisionist goals that are unlikely on the part of a rising power in a nuclear world, then, power preponderance is not necessary to ensure the ability of the United States to reassure its allies.

To be sure, power preponderance does present the advantage of allowing the unipole to command the commons—the high seas, airspace, and outer space (Posen 2003). But the value of controlling the commons depends on the strategy implemented by the state that possesses it. Specifically, command of the commons only presents significant benefits for a strategy aiming at further increasing the state's preponderance of power. Such a strategy, however, is likely to signal aggressive intentions, triggering balancing dynamics that render it self-defeating. In sum, power preponderance seems to be "much overrated" (Glaser 2011, 136).

* * *

In this essay, I have drawn inspiration from Jervis's *System Effects* to reflect on the value of systems thinking for some of the most important questions absorbing IR scholars and policymakers today. I conclude by summarizing what I think are the broader implications of his work for the conduct of IR scholarship and laying out three *futuribles*—three possible futures for systems thinking in IR.

Jervis's *System Effects* precludes simple theories or predictions; any mono-causal theory of anything social is bound to be of limited predictive power. We might be inclined to infer that social science—at least modern positivist social science, with its evolving standards of causal identification and its claim to describe and even predict the world—is nothing but a chimera. This would be too strong a reaction, however, and it would certainly not live up to the hopes Jervis himself expresses for his work.

Instead, we should proceed by implementing two principles. First, we should not abstain from studying politically important phenomena just because of the complications introduced by system effects, even if the latter preclude the use of the highest standards of causal identification. Second, we should tone down our claims about the predictive ability of any of our theories about phenomena that take place in a systemic context—as all the phenomena studied by IR do. Ideally, our theories will be able to show that when cause x is present, effect y is more likely. But when outcome y takes place within a system, system effects mean that many other interconnected, non-additive factors may condition it. We should therefore be cautious when extrapolating from one particular theory—focused on one particular dimension of a system—prescriptions about how outcomes are produced, as if they were produced in a vacuum. Instead, we should strive to articulate how other dimensions of the problem may condition our claims. The truth, or something thereabout, should emerge from our combined understanding of these different aspects of the issue at stake.

The role of IR is not to develop a field theory that accounts for every dimension of every problem in international relations. Rather, its role is to develop different theories, different languages, each dealing with different aspects of each problem in international relations. Along the lines of Richard Rorty's (1999) aspirations for philosophy, the goal of social science need not be to have fewer and fewer theories, with the regulative ideal of a single theory, a single language, with which we try to explain everything. Instead, our goal should be to produce ever more theories, more languages, to capture ever more dimensions of each politically important phenomenon. This "let a thousand flowers bloom" approach would be of great value for policy makers as well. If we take Jervis's view of complexity in social and political life seriously, the goal of describing any situation in international politics using one only theory is wrongheaded. Decision makers will be better informed about their context and better able to predict the outcome of their actions if they are supplied with multiple theories, each describing a particular aspect of the situational choice they face.

Since the fiftieth anniversary of the Cuban Missile Crisis is upon us as I write, let me use it to illustrate what I mean. Were we to send one representative of contemporary IR scholars in a time capsule to meet with President Kennedy in October 1962, we would not want her to prime the president in any single IR theory. No single theory would convey to the president the sum total of our usable knowledge in situations such as the one he faced. Instead, we would instruct our representative to brief JFK on a multiplicity of theories: deterrence theory, the spiral model, and nuclear-escalation dynamics; the psychological factors at play in crises, and other sources of misperceptions; the role played by audience costs, reputational concerns, the balance of power, etc. All of these were in play during the crisis, and none of them would in itself suffice to deal with the problem President Kennedy faced.

In the light of this modest aspiration, I foresee three possible scenarios for systems thinking in IR.

The first, more pessimistic possible future is one in which the trend towards higher causal identification standards acquires hegemonic proportions in political science, excluding systems thinking and any research on the complex system effects that Jervis did so much to emphasize. As a result, IR scholars interested in causal complexity and a systems approach would be pushed out of political science and, in all likelihood, into policy schools. This transformation would impoverish IR and our understanding of international politics. The study of system effects and complexity in international political life is an enterprise to which social theory is essential, and therefore it belongs squarely within social science. Any policy-oriented work should be seen as an implication, not the core, of our study of systems.

The second possible future is one in which system effects remain a niche specialty in IR, with most of the field tackling narrower questions that are amenable to the highest standards of causal identification but are usually less politically important. Since this outcome is the one that follows from the current situation of IR, I think it is the most likely to obtain. It would, however, be a future in which complex interactions and the role of emergent properties singled out in Jervis's *System Effects* would be scrutinized only by a minority of those studying IR, slowing down progress in our understanding of complexity in international politics.

The third, more optimistic scenario is one in which questions about system effects are again the object of a great deal of scholarship, and the complexity of international politics is fully embraced as a legitimate object of scientific study. For this future to materialize, two things would have to happen: political scientists in general would have to acknowledge that important political questions are plagued by system effects but must nonetheless continue to be studied with the best research designs to which they are amenable. And those interested in system effects more specifically would have to redouble their efforts to extract empirical implications, formulate testable hypotheses, and ultimately test their work using the available data.

Only from this concerted movement would we be able to maximize the potential Jervis saw for tackling complexity in social and political life.

NOTES

1. The expression is Jervis's, who borrows it from Hardin 1963, 80.
2. Throughout this essay, I adhere to the convention of using "IR" to refer to the discipline of International Relations and "international relations" to index its substantive domain of study.

3. My argument here is *not* that questions for which systems thinking is more useful tend to be questions on which we have limited available data. These two points are separate. That in international politics these two problems often go hand in hand does not imply any causal relation between the two statements.
4. Shapiro (2005) reaches a similar conclusion, calling for "problem-driven" rather than "method-driven" research.
5. For the sake of argument, I bracket the question of whether any type of research design can be guaranteed to do better in terms of causal identification. As I argue elsewhere (Monteiro and Ruby 2009), there are good reasons to be skeptical about any such foundational claims.
6. Glaser 2010 is a partial exception to this and, in this sense, truer to its systems-thinking credentials, as is its concomitant loss of parsimony and predictive power.

REFERENCES

Barkin, J. Samuel. 2010. *Realist Constructivism: Rethinking International Relations Theory*. Cambridge: Cambridge University Press.

Craig, Campbell. 2003. *Glimmer of a New Leviathan: Total War in the Realism of Niebhur, Morgenthau, and Waltz*. New York: Columbia University Press.

Debs, Alexandre, and Nuno Monteiro. 2012. "Known Unknowns: Power Shifts, Uncertainty, and War." *International Organization*, forthcoming.

Deudney, Daniel. 2011. "Unipolarity and Nuclear Weapons." In *International Relations Theory and the Consequences of Unipolarity*, ed. G. John Ikenberry, Michael Mastanduno, and William C. Wohlforth. Cambridge: Cambridge University Press.

Dunning, Thad. 2012. *Natural Experiments in the Social Sciences: A Design-Based Approach*. Cambridge: Cambridge University Press.

Fearon, James. 1995. "Rationalist Explanations for War." *International Organization* 49(3): 379–414.

Finnemore, Martha, and Kathryn Sikkink. 1998. "International Norm Dynamics and Political Change." *International Organization* 52(4): 887–917.

Gerber, Alan, and Donald Green. 2012. *Field Experiments: Design, Analysis, and Interpretation*. New York: W.W. Norton.

Giddens, Anthony. 1984. *The Constitution of Society: Outline of a Theory of Structuration*. Berkeley: University of California Press.

Glaser, Charles L. 2010. *Rational Theory of International Politics*. Princeton: Princeton University Press.

Glaser, Charles L. 2011. "Why Unipolarity Doesn't Matter (Much)." *Cambridge Review of International Affairs* 24(2): 135–47.

Hardin, Garrett. 1963. "The Cybernetics of Competition." *Perspectives in Biology and Medicine* 7: 58–84.

Hollis, Martin, and Steve Smith. 1990. *Explaining and Understanding in International Relations*. Oxford: Clarendon Press.

Jackson, Patrick, and Daniel Nexon. 1999. "Relations before States." *European Journal of International Relations* 5(3): 291–332.

Jervis, Robert. 1978. "Cooperation Under the Security Dilemma." *World Politics* 30(2): 167–214.

Jervis, Robert. 1989. *The Meaning of the Nuclear Revolution: Statecraft and the Prospect of Armageddon.* Ithaca, N.Y.: Cornell University Press.

Jervis, Robert. 1997. *System Effects: Complexity in Political and Social Life.* Princeton Princeton University Press.

Jervis, Robert. 2009. "Unipolarity: A Structural Perspective." *World Politics* 61(1): 188–213.

Keohane, Robert, ed. 1986. *Neorealism and Its Critics.* New York: Columbia University Press.

Koskenniemi, Martti. 2001. *The Gentle Civilizer of Nations: The Rise and Fall of International Law 1870–1960.* Cambridge: Cambridge University Press.

Little, Richard. 2007. *The Balance of Power in International Relations: Metaphors, Myths and Models.* New York: Cambridge University Press.

Mearsheimer, John. 2001. *The Tragedy of Great Power Politics.* New York: W.W. Norton.

Monteiro, Nuno. 2009. *Three Essays on Unipolarity.* Ph.D. diss., University of Chicago.

Monteiro, Nuno. 2011/2012. "Unrest Assured: Why Unipolarity Is Not Peaceful." *International Security* 36(3) (Winter): 9–40.

Monteiro, Nuno, and Alexandre Debs. 2012. "The Strategic Logic of Nuclear Proliferation." Yale University mimeo.

Monteiro, Nuno, and Keven Ruby. 2009. "IR and the False Promise of Philosophical Foundations." *International Theory* 1(1): 15–48.

Morrow, James. 1994. "Alliances, Credibility, and Peacetime Costs." *Journal of Conflict Resolution* 38(2): 270–97.

Nexon, Daniel. 2009. "The Balance of Power in the Balance." *World Politics* 61(2): 330–59.

Pepinsky, Thomas. 2005. "From Agents to Outcomes: Simulation in International Relations." *European Journal of International Relations* 11(3): 367–94.

Posen, Barry. 2003. "Command of the Commons: The Military Foundation of U.S. Hegemony." *International Security* 28(13): 5–46.

Pouliot, Vincent. 2008. "The Logic of Practicality: A Theory of Practice of Security Communities." *International Organization* 62(2): 257–88.

Powell, Robert. 2006. "War as a Commitment Problem." *International Organization* 60(1): 169–203.

Rorty, Richard. 1999. *Philosophy and Social Hope.* London: Penguin.

Russett, Bruce. 1969. "The Young Science of International Politics." *World Politics* 22(1): 87–94.

Schelling, Thomas. 1960. *The Strategy of Conflict.* Cambridge, Mass: Harvard University Press.

Schelling, Thomas. 1966. *Arms and Influence.* New Haven: Yale University Press.

Schmidt, Brian. 2002. "On the History and Historiography of International Relations." In *Handbook of International Relations*, ed. Walter Carlsnaes, Thomas Risse and Beth A. Simmons. London: Sage.

Sechser, Todd. 2010. "Goliath's Curse: Coercive Threats and Asymmetric Power." *International Organization* 64(4): 627–60.

Shapiro, Ian. 2005. *The Flight From Reality in the Human Sciences*. Princeton: Princeton University Press.

Snidal, Duncan. 1985. "The Limits of Hegemonic Stability Theory." *International Organization* 39(4): 579–614.

Waltz, Kenneth. 1979. *Theory of International Politics*. New York: McGraw Hill.

Webster, Murray, and Jane Sell, eds. 2007. *Laboratory Experiments in the Social Sciences*. Burlington, Mass.: Elsevier.

Wendt, Alexander. 1999. *Social Theory of International Politics*. Cambridge: Cambridge University Press.

Wohlforth, William. 1999. "The Stability of a Unipolar World." *International Security* 24(1): 5–41.

Richard A. Posner

JERVIS ON COMPLEXITY THEORY

ABSTRACT: *The correct solution to complex problems, such as those involved in international relations, can generally be discovered ex post but not predicted ex ante. Economics and game theory attempt to model such complexity, but have difficulty taking into account psychological subtleties, the myriad factors that each agent considers when making a decision, and cultural differences. And understanding that one is dealing with a system—that is, with interacting factors instead of with insulated monads—may not make the questions any more amenable to prediction, particularly because the more unique an event, the less likely it is to be foreseen. Jervis's analysis of complex systems may therefore be more of a contribution to the historical sciences than to predictive social science.*

System Effects: Complexity in Political and Social Life (Princeton University Press, 1997), by Robert Jervis, is an excellent introduction to complexity theory—or, equivalently, systems analysis—despite its rather narrow focus on international conflict, mainly war.

It is important to distinguish between difficulty and complexity. A question can be difficult without being complex; it can be an ethical or values question, or simply a question to which no answer can be given for want of data. A question is complex when it is difficult by virtue of involving complicated interactions, or, in other words, when it arises

---

Judge Richard A. Posner, U.S. Court of Appeals for the Seventh Circuit, senior lecturer at University of Chicago Law School, is the author, most recently, of the eighth edition of *Economic Analysis of Law* (Aspen Publishers, 2011).

from a system rather than from a monad. The system can be economic—a market, for example, involving interactions among sellers and between sellers and buyers. It can be ecological—a population of animals that compete to maximize (unconsciously, of course) their genetic fitness. It can be a cellphone or other complex machine, the cells of a living body, the subatomic particles that compose an atom, the solar system.

International Relations as a Complex System

The system that Jervis emphasizes is the international community—a system of competing nation states. This is an immensely complicated system, in part because each state is a complex system; in part because of pervasive uncertainty; in part because of the complexity of human psychology; and in part because of the complicating effect of strategic interaction (found also in markets): In deciding on an action involving another nation-state, a government must try to anticipate the reaction of the other nation-state, and in trying to anticipate that reaction, it must reckon with the fact that the reaction will depend, in part, on how that other state believes that the state that initiates the action will in turn react to the reaction.

Unsurprisingly, given these sources of complexity, the decisions made by the participants in the system of nation states that is the international community are frequently found *ex post* to be mistaken. Jervis gives countless examples. I will mention just one. Before World War I, Britain and Germany might have seemed natural allies, because they had a long history of friendly relations and no basis for serious conflicts. Britain and France, in contrast, had a continuing history of disputes, mainly because of competing colonial ambitions. But because of these disputes, and because Russia and France were allied, and because Britain didn't want to find itself at war with both Russia and France, Britain decided to patch up its disagreements with France. So Britain and France became allies. Since Germany and France were enemies, Britain's alliance with France turned Germany against Britain, and Britain and Germany became enemies even though they had no serious underlying sources of conflict. This is a relatively simple example of how a system, because of the interactions of its parts, can generate perverse results that are unlikely to be anticipated.

Complexity and Complexity Theory

While I have characterized Jervis's book as a book about complexity theory or systems analysis (which I regard as different terms for the same thing), I am not sure how useful this description is. In the fifteen years since Jervis's book was published, terms such as *complexity theory*, *systems analysis*, *system analysis*, and *analysis of complex systems* have come to be used, not as Jervis uses such terms, but instead to describe various analytical methodologies in mathematics, science, and engineering. Thus, none of the italicized terms appear in the index to *System Effects*, and while there are index entries for "complexity" and "system," they are very few. As far as I have been able to determine, Jervis has not written further on the subject of complexity theory or systems analysis, though he has remained a prolific contributor to the literature of international relations. The field to which his work is a major contribution—well named by his subtitle: "Complexity in Political and Social Life"—has moved on, but Jervis's book remains a landmark well worth reading and study.

In contrast to "complexity theory" per se, Jervis describes no specific analytical method. Essentially the book is a series of case studies, in which outcomes are related to anticipations, interactions, assumptions, communications, information (and especially lack thereof), misunderstandings, and mistakes. The point of the book is to show that, given these sources of complexity, outcomes are difficult to predict and therefore are often mispredicted, resulting in disappointment or disaster.

I don't mean to criticize Jervis's approach because of its lack of formalism or rigor; it seems in fact the right approach to take to the historical situations to which Jervis applies it. I think it can be applied fruitfully to other conflict situations as well, especially political conflicts, and more broadly to any conflict situation characterized by uncertainty.

I am thinking of uncertainty in the Frank Knight (1921) and John Maynard Keynes (1921) sense—a situation in which numerical probabilities cannot be attached to the alternative outcomes. When World War II began, it would have been possible for an observer to list possible outcomes but impossible for anyone to attach a responsible numerical probability to any outcome that appeared realistic (as opposed to the zero probability that, for example, the Danish army would repulse a German invasion of Denmark).

Complexity and Ignorance

Uncertainty is common when information is limited and decisions depend on a circle of mutual anticipation of reactions. Take the stock market: A speculator bases his trading decisions on an anticipation of how other traders will trade, knowing that their decisions may be influenced by their anticipation of what *he* will do, and so his anticipation will in turn be influenced by his estimate of their anticipations, and their decisions may in turn be influenced by what they think he will think they are anticipating that he will do. Keynes compared the stock market to a beauty contest in which the winner is the one who guesses correctly which contestant will receive the most votes. Jervis's analysis could also be applied to negotiations over the purchase of a business or the terms of settlement of a lawsuit, which are both examples of conflict under uncertainty.

There are ways of formally modeling such situations: The principal ways are game theory and economics. Game theory deals explicitly with strategic situations. Economics, when defined as the study of rational choice rather than (as used to be the case) the study of explicit economic markets, could be thought to include game theory as a special case; and in fact economists use game theory extensively. The economic example sketched earlier presents a typical set of interactions of rational actors in an economic market, but it is easy to see how the same analysis could be applied to a similar set of interactions in a nonmarket situation—indeed, in any situation in which interacting rational actors have conflicting interests.

But I can see why Jervis would not think either game theory or economics a key to understanding the strategic situations on which his book focuses (there are a few index references to game theory, none to economics or economic theory). The conflict situations he analyzes involve pervasive uncertainty in highly politicized settings. Uncertainty engenders psychological reactions that may be rational but hard to model; for example, a rational response to uncertainty is simply to freeze—to do nothing—in the hope that the uncertainty will be dispelled over time by receipt of new information; in other words, by seeing how things work out. Political interactions tend also to be difficult to model because of the variety of considerations that influence a political actor. And whenever one is dealing with cross-country data, the need to adjust for cultural and other differences makes interpretation difficult.

Jervis's approach is analytical and informed by data, although not quantitative data, but the analysis is informal, and that may be dictated by the subject matter of his study.

The Asymmetrical Usefulness of Complexity Analysis

The $64 question about the book, however, is whether careful reading and study of it by decision makers—whether in government dealing with foreign-policy issues such as those that Jervis's book discusses, or in business (negotiating deals) or in law (conducting adversary proceedings or negotiating settlements)—would lead to better decisions. Complexity theory is undoubtedly useful for solving scientific problems, but how useful is it for solving problems of human society?

There is no indication that it has led to better decisions, if one thinks of all the foreign-policy, military, political, natural-catastrophe-related, and economic blunders of the past fifteen years. The financial crisis of 2008 is exemplary. It appears to have been the result of ignorance; complacency on the part of economists; political incentives and interactions; extraordinarily complex financial instruments; and complicated interactions among regulators and bankers, lenders and borrowers, and members of the worldwide financial industry. Could careful study of Jervis's book by bankers, regulators, and politicians have headed off the collapse? Probably not.

There is a big difference between the reconstruction of causality after an accident or other untoward event, on the one hand, and, on the other hand, using that reconstruction to make a prediction that allows the next untoward event to be prevented. Reconstruction that identifies a single historical cause of a problem—say a design defect in a machine that caused it to malfunction—enables prevention. But reconstruction that reveals causality resulting from unique interactions may have no predictive/preventive value at all.

Maybe what is needed is not more failure stories, but more success stories. But I suspect that what the success stories would show is that good results can be expected when the circumstances are not terribly complex. Rain is forecasted, so you carry an umbrella, and as a result you don't get drenched. There is a reliable prediction even though it contains an error term, and there is a cheap method of preventing the predicted event from causing harm; because it is cheap, the fact that the prediction may be incorrect is not a deterrent to taking the precaution. As one "complexifies" the circumstances up to the level encountered in the financial markets in the 2000s, radical ignorance—uncertainty in the Knight-Keynes sense—thwarts prevention.

The moral may be to try to keep things simple. That may be good advice for financial regulators; the banking industry can be forced to simplify. It is infeasible for foreign affairs. So maybe the correct understanding of Jervis's book is as a contribution to history, not to social science.

I do not want to leave the impression that complexity defies rigorous analysis, the kind of analysis one finds in mathematics, the natural sciences, and social sciences such as game theory and economics. There are many complex systems in nature that science has analyzed successfully—the weather system is immensely complex but quite well understood. The global economic system is immensely complex, but economics has had at least partial success in analyzing it. Game theory made a contribution to maintaining the "balance of terror" during the Cold War, a precarious but nevertheless durable equilibrium (albeit with occasional interruptions).

The problem is not complexity per se but the inability to understand the interactions among the component parts of a complex system. Political scientists and other social scientists are not able to understand the interactions that take place in conflict situations in international affairs, except in terms too general to have much predictive or preventive value. Jervis analyzes the complex origins of historical crises, but not with models to which new crises can be fitted, enabling reliable prediction or effective preventive action.

Andrea Jones-Rooy and Scott Page (2012) emphasize advances in complexity theory as applied to social life since Jervis's book was published. Yet they confirm rather than undermine my suggestion that, thus far, the application of complexity theory to social life has produced retrospective rather than prospective illumination. They acknowledge that often "while we may be unable to predict the outcomes of some complex systems, *ex post* we can make sense of them." They go on to illustrate the point with striking examples, such as the financial crisis and Arab Spring and Facebook, of failure to anticipate the "phase transitions" that characterize social life. The term is from physics, and refers to the fact that dramatic transformations (for example of H_2O from liquid to solid) can be triggered by minute environmental changes.

However, physicists understand phase transitions in nature well enough to make predictions about them. Social scientists understand them in human society only well enough to explain them after they have happened.

REFERENCES

Jervis, Robert. 1997. *System Effects: Complexity in Political and Social Life*. Princeton: Princeton University Press.
Jones-Rooy, Andrea, and Scott Page. 2012. "The Complexity of System Effects." *Critical Review* 24(3): 313–42.
Keynes, John Maynard. 1921. *A Treatise on Probability*. London: Macmillan.
Knight, Frank H. 1921. "Risk, Uncertainty, and Profit." Boston, Mass.: Houghton Mifflin Co.

Philip E. Tetlock, Michael C. Horowitz, and Richard Herrmann

SHOULD "SYSTEMS THINKERS" ACCEPT THE LIMITS ON POLITICAL FORECASTING OR PUSH THE LIMITS?

ABSTRACT: *Historical analysis and policy making often require counterfactual thought experiments that isolate hypothesized causes from a vast array of historical possibilities. However, a core precept of Jervis's "systems thinking" is that causes are so interconnected that the historian can only with great difficulty imagine causation by subtracting all variables but one. Prediction, according to Jervis, is even more problematic: The more sensitive an event is to initial conditions (e.g., butterfly effects), the harder it is to derive accurate forecasts. Nevertheless, if awareness of system effects can help forecasters better calibrate their probability estimates of whether or not certain events will come to pass, systems thinkers who are pessimistic about prediction are diluting their confidence too much. The challenge is a meta-cognitive one: thinking systematically about when to engage in systems thinking; and weighing the costs and benefits of using simple*

Philip E. Tetlock is professor of management, Wharton School, Management Department, University of Pennsylvania; Michael C. Horowitz is an associate professor in the Department of Political Science, University of Pennsylvania; and Richard Herrmann is the director of the Mershon Center for International Security Studies, The Ohio State University.

This research was supported by a research contract to the University of Pennsylvania and the University of California from the Intelligence Advanced Research Projects Activity (IARPA) via the Department of Interior National Business Center, contract D11PC20061. The U.S. Government is authorized to reproduce and distribute reprints for Government purposes notwithstanding any copyright annotation thereon. Disclaimer: The views and conclusions expressed herein are those of the authors and should not be interpreted as necessarily representing the official policies or endorsements, either expressed or implied, of IARPA, DoI/NBC, or the U.S. Government.

or complex heuristics in policy environments that can shift suddenly from quiescence to turbulence.

Robert Jervis has long had a keen eye for our collective blind spots. In *Perception and Misperception in International Politics* (1976), he documented how easily policy makers slip into lazy, self-serving patterns of reasoning. In *System Effects: Complexity in Political and Social Life* (Princeton University Press, 1997), he explored the complexity of social systems and the potential for unexpected consequences when policy makers fail to do the hard mental labor of tracing interconnections among causes and effects (Jervis 1997, 29). Thus, Jervis challenges our ability to make sensible political choices. And the challenge cannot be overcome simply by thinking about it. As Daniel Kahneman confesses in *Thinking, Fast and Slow* (2011), despite forty years of research on cognitive biases, his initial ("system 1") instincts still lead him into the same traps. Apparently there are no quick consciousness-raising fixes.

We suspect that Jervis is fundamentally right: System effects are subtle, pervasive, and potent shapers of political outcomes. And people tend to underestimate the subtlety, ubiquity, and potency of system effects. Most of us are too quick to embrace simple models of causation that are less cognitively taxing than the intricate negative- or positive-feedback-loop models of causation underlying the hurly-burly of events swirling about us.

Our essay will explore the seemingly gloomy implications of the Jervisian worldview for a core requirement of rationality: our ability to predict the connections between policy actions and outcomes. We agree that the implications are often depressing. But there is a real possibility—a hypothesis worth testing—that encouraging systems thinking will boost forecasting accuracy under circumscribable conditions.

We expect pushback from at least two philosophical camps. Readers of an objectivist or pragmatic bent may suspect that we are trying to repackage as controversial an obvious and non-controversial hypothesis. All knowledge rests on relationships between causes and effects that we identify through the explanation of effects, and that we test through prediction. When a prediction is confirmed, we become more confident in both the reliability of forecaster and the explanatory framework that produced the prediction; when a prediction fails, we dial back our confidence. The "systemic" nature of the political world no more precludes confidence in predictions than does that of the natural world.

Readers of a relativist bent, however, will suspect that we have taken on an impossible task. Philosophers have repeatedly shown that there is no simple correspondence between explanation and prediction (Suppe 1977). After all, elegant explanations may not yield accurate predictions (e.g., geophysical models of earthquakes), while profoundly flawed explanations can generate surprisingly accurate predictions (e.g., pre-Copernican geocentric models of the night sky). In the dissociationist view of explanation and prediction, deriving accurate predictions from systemic explanations of social phenomena will prove as frustrating as predicting earthquakes, since knowing that something is a system does not make it any easier to predict.

We stake out a middle ground between the tight coupling of explanation and prediction and their total severance: what we call "loose coupling." We agree with dissociationists that there is no guarantee that sound systems thinking will translate into better political forecasting and no guarantee that the best political forecasters will be sound systems thinkers. And we agree with common-sense objectivists that the smart money in any forecasting tournament should be on those whose mental models of the world best fit the complexities of the world. That said, we also see money to be made by taking even-odds bets from both dissociationists (who underestimate the predictive advantage conferred by systems thinking) and objectivists (who overestimate the benefits of systems thinking).

To illustrate the difficulty of the underlying issues, we offer the following thought experiment. Imagine a large group of intelligence analysts, all committed Jervisians, who are tasked with monitoring trends around the globe. Also imagine—and this is really a stretch—that we have gold-standard metrics for judging the fruits of their analytical labors. We have retrospective metrics that allow us to assess the accuracy of the "lessons from history" that analysts draw—so we can unravel such classic counterfactual mysteries as whether there were missed opportunities in 1954 or 1963 for resolving the Cold War far earlier than happened, or missed opportunities in 1967 for achieving a durable Arab-Israeli peace that has still yet to happen. And we have prospective metrics that allow us to gauge the accuracy of the Jervisian analysts' likelihood judgments of well-specified futures, such as whether the eurozone will fragment in 2013 or whether the Chinese polity will evolve into a multi-party democracy by 2017.

Can we, even under these ideal conditions, determine whether Jervisian analysts do a better job on our gold-standard metrics than analysts untutored in systems thinking? Even with the miracle metrics, answers will be elusive. For what exactly do we mean by "a better job"? We presumably don't mean "better" on all possible questions we might pose. Some questions will be so easy that all analysts would get them right. And others will be so hard, laden with "irreducible uncertainty," that any improvement would be impossible.

In order to distinguish luck from skill, the questions we ask our Jervisian experts would have to be in the "Goldilocks zone of difficulty." We would also need an adequate number of questions to enable the law of large numbers to kick in (Mauboussin 2012). Armed with the miracle metrics yielded by such a method, we can revisit our question: Would Jervisian thinking improve predictive accuracy?

We doubt that Jervis is so radical a dissociationist that he would bet that systems thinking confers no advantage. And we doubt that he sees explanation and prediction as being so tightly coupled as to justify an aggressive-odds bet on systems thinking conferring a big advantage. Jervis probably falls somewhere in the middle—as do we. We suspect he is more pessimistic than we are about the predictive benefits of systems thinking, but more optimistic than the dissociationists.

The rest of our essay will, first, lay out the Jervisian grounds for pessimism. We then make the case for conditional optimism and sketch some approaches that might yield incremental predictive improvements.

Grounds for Epistemic Pessimism

Accepting the central arguments of *System Effects* means acknowledging nontrivial limits on predictability in world politics. These limits include the complications inherent in conceptualizing and operationalizing key causal concepts; the fact that most causal claims are limited by scope conditions and hinge on interactions; the fact that messy mixes of self-fulfilling and self-negating prophecies are often at work; and the complexity of envisioning counterfactuals.

Concepts and measures: The principle of sensitive dependence on initial conditions—dubbed "butterfly effects" by complexity theorists—posits that, even if we had predictively powerful laws of world politics, we often could not apply these laws because we cannot measure sufficiently precisely whether the on-the-ground antecedent conditions for activating them had been satisfied. The best-informed observers disagree over key issues such as the rationality of the Iranian leadership, the stability of the North Korean regime, and whether insolvent states in the eurozone will accept German-dictated austerity terms or whether the German public will tolerate what it sees as financial free riders.

Further, as Jervis (1997, 74) points out, simple "power" explanations will not do, because core concepts like power are so embedded in the relationships of a given system that their measurement is fraught with controversy and error. Not only is power relational, resting on a host of assumptions about the capabilities of others, it is also multidimensional, with no agreed-on formula for aggregating components. Moreover, Jervis (ibid., 191–95) shows that predictions depend on additional assumptions about the alternatives available to an actor, the expected behavior of third parties, and how trends in relative capabilities shape each side's expectations about future relationships. Such complexities tend to decouple power explanations from the ability to make predictions about power relationships.

Conditions and interactions: Jervis (1997, 239) quotes his former faculty adviser at Berkeley, Kenneth Waltz, that the theory of power politics works best "when the game of power politics is really played hard." But it is not always played hard. Even at the height of the Cold War, as Jervis shows, the great powers behaved in ways that often made geostrategic sense only when viewed through very particular sets of ideological lenses. Combat operations in systemically peripheral areas such as Vietnam and Angola were expensive but had minuscule effects on the balance of power. At the time, Hans Morgenthau attributed these policies to nationalist crusading, almost the opposite of power politics. Today, prominent advocates of the power-politics perspective complain that domestic lobbies and misguided understandings of both material interests and morality drive United States policy in the Middle East (Mearsheimer and Walt 2007). Jervis (1997, 118–19) does not miss the irony of believing in the predictive value of a theory that repeatedly fails to predict the foreign policy of the most important power in the system.

When Jervis explains great-power behavior in the periphery of the world system, he concentrates on dominoes, feedback loops, and conflict spirals. From his early work on, Jervis has viewed signaling and communication as far more complicated than simple message-sent/message-received models. And when we allow for the impact of divergent prior beliefs, different assumptions about what even constitutes a signal, and messier inferential leaps, our ability to map out even the *possible* routes the interaction may take comes into question. Predicting which course history will take starts looking foolish. For Jervis (1997, 171–74), dominoes and spirals follow no linear logic. Too much hinges on quirky human perceptions of structural constraints.

Human expectations: Policy makers not only have different starting assumptions about what is at stake, they also coordinate their expectations and update their thinking differently as history unfolds. For instance, it is hard to say when historical animosities will overwhelm contemporary calculations. Many analysts assume that old grudges will keep China and Japan apart for a long time, and perhaps South Korea and Japan too, although countervailing geostrategic considerations could prevail. South Korea's last-minute reversal of a decision to sign a new intelligence-sharing agreement with Japan in June 2012, however, demonstrates that historical sensitivities—and the domestic politics they trigger—matter. For Jervis, identifying the competing considerations is important, but much easier than determining which ones will carry the day. The forecaster must not only weigh the tradeoffs, but predict the political actors' strategic calculations during each possible iteration of the game they think they are playing.

The deceptively simple guess-the-number game illustrates the degree to which indeterminacy is woven into the fabric of the social world (Nagel 1995). Suppose you ask students at your local university to guess a number between zero and 100 with the goal that their guesses come as close as possible to two-thirds of the average guess of their classmates. If your class has not been tutored in game theory, the likely guess will be close to 33. They will tacitly assume that other students will randomly select numbers between zero and 100, which will average up to 50; two-thirds of 50 is roughly 33. If your class has been tutored in game theory—a key form of systems thinking—the likely guess will be closer to the Nash equilibrium answer of zero. The students will recognize that their classmates will have initially thought through the answer to 33, and that two-thirds of 33 is approximately 22. But they will also recognize that their fellow students will follow through this chain of reasoning and adjust their answer accordingly until they converge toward zero. Of course, the technically correct game-theoretic answer is not necessarily the empirically correct answer (it is possible to be too clever by half). If the class is divided between game-theory naïfs and game-theory sophisticates, the correct answer will probably fall somewhere between 33 and zero, say, 16. And the correct answer will change as people make new estimates about each other's learning curves—and as new people either enter or exit the system.

In this game, the players have no ideological baggage or special axes to grind. In world politics, they typically do. Jervis (1997, 230–32) reminds us that policy makers often default into the view that good (or bad) things go together, making it easy for emotions to drive analysis. Policy makers sample information in biased ways; their conclusions about an identical action may depend on whether it was carried out by someone they like or someone they don't; and they apply different moral standards when dealing with a friend or enemy—rationalizing their actions by delegitimizing their adversaries. Moreover, an emotional charge can shape an agent's interpretation of the strategic context or assumptions about how many iterations the other agents will be thinking about. Incorporating these additional possibilities in forecasting could improve accuracy but might well induce analysis-paralysis.

Simple complexity. Although Jervis identifies psychological obstacles to accurate prediction, his cautionary message runs deeper. And the problem goes beyond people not being smart enough. The world is often just too complex to predict.

Capturing the multiplicity of interacting causal streams may also be made harder by our compartmentalized, departmentalized systems of higher education. Jervis worries that too much professional training in hypothesis testing emphasizes holding all else constant and concentrating on a particular factor: "Much thinking about causation, in science and everyday life, assumes the possibility of comparing two situations that are identical, except for one factor. If we could achieve this ideal state of affairs, we could attribute any differences in the outcome to the difference in the state of the one element. That is why, in non-experimental social science, we encourage our students to choose cases in which ceteris paribus holds." But, as Garrett Hardin (1963, 83) puts it, in a system "we can never do merely one thing."

Physicians routinely recognize this latent complexity whenever they prescribe a drug. But they can consult side-effect and drug-interaction checklists in computerized databases. In world politics, there is no equivalent of the *Physician's Desk Reference*—and even smart policy makers slip into embarrassingly crude analogical reasoning of the form:

"If it worked out this way over there, it will probably do the same over here."

To appreciate the difficulties in understanding politics, consider this politically charged exercise in historical what-iffery: Suppose all the major powers in pre-World War II Europe had possessed nuclear weapons, with a guaranteed second-strike capability. Would war have still broken out? The thought experiment puts advocates of aggressive preemption of the Iranian nuclear program on the defensive. If they answer "no," they accept that even Hitler was deterrable, which raises the possibility that the Iranian mullahs are also deterrable. If they answer "yes," they put themselves in an implausible historical box. They have to argue not just that Hitler was a risk taker but a suicidally reckless one, yet there is a lot of evidence that Hitler calibrated his risk taking in the 1930s quite methodically.

But a motivated systems thinker can crank up the analytical microscope to neutralize any dissonant counterfactual thought experiment. The preceding thought experiment, like most in world politics (Tetlock and Belkin 1996), is contestable on a host of grounds. And a good systems thinker will quickly seize on co-tenability objections that spotlight how problematic it is to change only one thing. One could make a good case that a multipolar nuclearized state system would never have allowed as radically revisionist a regime as the Third Reich to come to power—or that a pre-World War II Europe as technologically advanced as the one in the thought experiment would also have been much wealthier, making the rise of extremism far less likely. Looking forward in time, Kenneth Waltz (2012) argues that the Iranian acquisition of nuclear weapons in a multipolar nuclearized Middle East would stabilize the system rather than upending it. In this conditional-forecasting exercise, Waltz tacitly assumes that everything else can be held constant. The only change is the addition of nuclear weapons. In a system, however, that is a precarious assumption. The effect that Iran's acquisition of nuclear weapons would have on other actors, their domestic politics, and their readiness to engage in conflict of various sorts needs to be spelled out. We suspect that, in this context, systems thinking is likely to lead to policy agnosticism. Making predictions in the face of such complexity requires a degree of dogmatism, and a "dogmatic Jervisian" is oxymoronic.

The idea that predictability is limited implies that it will be impossible for analysts already performing at the optimal forecasting frontier to reduce their "misses" or false negatives without simultaneously increasing their false positives. They will not be able to identify a coming financial crisis, nuclear holocaust, or genocide without also predicting many disasters that do not actually happen. Indeed, the more effective the intelligence agency, the greater its risk of ensnarement in a systemic predicament known as accountability ping-pong: As improving accuracy becomes increasingly impossible, the only way the agency can appease the external constituencies to which it is answerable is to shift its tolerance threshold for making one or another type of error (Tetlock and Mellers 2011). One "learns" to avoid only the most recent mistake. If intelligence analysts have just been raked over the coals for underestimating country x's nuclear program, they may overestimate the nuclear capabilities of country y.

Grounds for Conditional Optimism

Although Jervis understands the logic of accountability ping-pong and the fact that those skeptical about the possibility of boosting aggregate accuracy (hits minus false alarms) will sometimes be right, his work with the intelligence community implies that he sees a non-negligible probability that the skeptics might sometimes be wrong. Jervis (2010) has worked with the intelligence community to help it learn from mistakes in National Intelligence Estimates. Here we are in deep agreement. It would be worse to make the mistake of giving up prematurely when there is potential for improvement than to make the mistake of trying to do the impossible. While Jervis is not optimistic about accurate forecasting, his arguments about pervasive system effects in world politics are not incompatible with there being substantial pockets of predictability in world politics.

We see at least three possible reasons for cautious optimism. First, systems thinking can help forecasters avoid the mistake that has traditionally taken the greatest toll on their accuracy: overconfident theory-driven reasoning (Tetlock 2005). Second, systems thinking leads us to tools for monitoring our own reasoning and nudging us toward normatively defensible modes of thinking (Kahneman's [2011] System 2 thinking). Third, systems thinking can sensitize us to the advantages of exploring alternative methods of combining diverse perspectives through such techniques as competing prediction teams, aggregation algorithms, and prediction markets.

Restraining overconfident theory-driven reasoning: Rival theories of how social systems operate often drove disagreements among the political forecasters examined in *Expert Political Judgment* (Tetlock 2005), and they continue to drive disputes in a new, much larger-scale prediction tournament currently sponsored by the Intelligence Advanced Research Projects Activity (IARPA). Considerable field and laboratory research suggests that the best antidote to runaway theorizing is more sophisticated systems thinking that acknowledges countervailing variables and gaps in our understanding of how they interact (Keil 2010; Tetlock and Mellers 2011). We go out on a limb by including examples of the perils of overconfidence from ongoing IARPA forecasting problems to which no one knew the answers at the time this was written. There is a non-negligible probability that some of our most opinionated forecasters would be proven right on any given issue—undercutting the superficial prescriptive thrust of our argument, but highlighting our deeper point about the probabilistic nature of the linkages between "good analytical process" and "good outcomes" in world politics.

1. The likelihood of at least one country leaving the eurozone by April 1, 2013. One cluster of forecasters—game-theoretic systems thinkers—offers a bold hedgehog-style forecast, a 0.9-plus probability of at least one exit. In this view, the crisis boils down to a simple arithmetic equation: How much is Germany prepared to pay to keep debtor states such as Greece, Italy, and Spain in the eurozone? If the retention costs exceed German willingness to pay, defections become inevitable. The key parties are caught in a positive feedback loop of mutual frustration that will culminate in a relationship-rupturing temper tantrum. Another cluster of forecasters—more eclectic or fox-style in their theorizing—offers a more tentative forecast, wobbling between .35 and .65. They note systemic forces that could put the brakes on the conflict spiral. The more frustrated mass opinion becomes, the more elites are reminded of the shared values that inspired the eurozone in the first place. The hedgehog forecasters give virtually zero weight to these cultural-institutional braking mechanisms, but they might prove right in this case (it would be difficult for any point of view in the marketplace of ideas to survive if it were always wrong). The most we can say is that, based on research to date, one is better off betting on the more eclectic system analysis that incorporates both positive and negative feedback loops.

2. The likelihood of the value of the euro falling below $1.20 before January 1, 2013 (a now-resolved question). Forecasters in the IARPA tournament are likelier to do better if they recognize the interconnections among questions. A falling euro could save the eurozone if it permits currently insolvent countries to export their way back to economic health. But there is opposition in northern Europe to running the monetary printing press at top speed. The parties are engaged in a delicate political-economic balancing act. The Germans want to keep up the pressure for massive internal reform in debtor countries, but they don't want the resulting pain to be so acute that it causes major defections from the eurozone. There needs to be sustained, long-term infliction of pain (hence the crude cartoon depictions in Greek newspapers of Angela Merkel as a neo-Nazi dominatrix)—but not too much pain. The pain also must be understood as the means for catalyzing economic reform, not as an end in itself. So, if the euro is going to fall, it should fall slowly (it should not be too obvious that the eurozone is monetizing debt). Also, there is the broader international monetary system to consider. If the euro fell too fast, it could trigger competitive devaluations by the United States and other major economic powers. Our best IARPA tournament forecasters put a high probability on the euro falling below $1.20 but refrained from going all the way to 1.0 because they recognized the braking mechanisms as well.

3. The identity of the Socialist challenger in the 2012 election for the presidency of France (a now-resolved question). Once upon a time, the smart money favored Dominique Strauss-Kahn (DSK) as the next socialist candidate for the Presidency of France—and an even-odds shot at defeating the incumbent, Nicolas Sarkozy. But DSK's private life was problematic even by French standards. After an incident with a maid in New York City and subsequent revelations, his career cratered. It would be absurd to expect forecasters to have predicted the specifics of his undoing, but it is not absurd to expect shrewd forecasters to temper their bets given the inherent instability in private lives and the skill of opposition researchers. The best forecasters know that stochastic systems are embedded within stochastic systems, like Russian dolls, and that micro forces in mostly invisible lower systems can suddenly have macro consequences. It would be an exaggeration to call these eruptions "black swans," because they were not inherently unpredictable. It is more appropriate to call them grey swans because they fall in

the zone of barely detectible possibilities we cannot fully articulate but sense are worth thinking about.

In all of these examples, the more Jervisian the thinker, the more moderate were his or her probability estimates. Although moderation is not an inevitable consequence of systems thinking (systems thinkers can posit positive feedback loops so strong that they produce high-confidence forecasts of change, or negative feedback loops so strong that they produce high-confidence predictions of stasis), moderation is probably a common consequence (Tetlock 2005). Given the evidence of widespread overconfidence on difficult diagnostic problems, this moderation-of-probability effect may be sufficient justification for translating scholarly analysis into practical guidance. There is, however, the risk that excessive systems thinking will lead to underconfidence, which is just one more tradeoff that managers of any intelligence community have to manage.

Tools that help us think more methodically: Another potential benefit of systems thinking is its emphasis on acknowledging causal complexity and cultivating a capacity to respond nimbly to new configurations of forces. A strong candidate for inclusion as a "thinking guideline" in a Jervisian checklist for intelligence analysts is: Never make unconditional forecasts (likelihood of Y) without unpacking the conditions bearing on the target event (x_1, x_2, ...) and entering them into a series of conditional forecasts ($p(y/x_1)$, $p(y/x_2)$, ...)). For research suggests that initial gut-level probability estimates that people offer in response to unconditional-forecasting questions often stray far from the deliberative estimates they would have offered if they had worked through the probabilities of key causal antecedents being in place, the conditional probabilities of the target outcome conditional on each antecedent being in place, and each combination of antecedents being in place (Tetlock 2005, ch. 4).

It is, however, still an open empirical question whether rapid-fire "blink" forecasts are more accurate, less accurate, or as accurate as forecasts derived from the painfully deliberative process of working through all possible combinations. There are clashing schools of thought on the pros and cons of simple versus complex heuristics. For our part, we bet on the benefits of "disciplined complexity." And there are technologies, such as Bayesian inference software, that now make such deliberation feasible within reasonable time/effort constraints—so there is no longer any good excuse for not undertaking them.

Extracting the wisdom from a crowd: Over the last few decades, scholars have identified myriad methods of distilling composite forecasts from individuals, ranging from the Delphi technique (for eliciting views of each group member while minimizing conformity distortions) to prediction markets (in which participants second guess each other's bets on possible futures) to purely statistical forms of machine learning that continually experiment with new combinations of predictors, with the unchanging goal of minimizing squared error (Armstrong 2006). These aggregation techniques often yield substantially more accurate forecasting than the forecasts of individual forecasters and even the unweighted averages of their forecasts (a tough benchmark to beat [Surowiecki 2005]). And this is exactly what a Jervisian would expect. Aggregating perspectives should be most helpful when observers at different vantage points can pick up different tiny bits of the truth; that is, when no observer has a vantage point that allows him to see the entire system (including its subsystems) at work.

Even though these aggregation techniques work well, they aren't perfect, and their imperfections are sometimes misunderstood to be proof that they don't work at all. Consider the flurry in prediction markets to anticipate how the Supreme Court would rule on the Affordable Care Act. In theory, prediction markets harness not only the wisdom of crowds, but the systematic competition between market participants, incentivized by rewards to make the best possible guesses. The current trading price on the prediction market is supposed to be the best possible estimate of the probability of the target event—and just prior to the Supreme Court decision, one leading prediction market attached a 75-percent probability to the possibility that the individual-insurance mandate would be overturned. However, the conservative Chief Justice, John Roberts, treated the individual mandate to have health insurance not as a penalty but as a tax—and upheld the law as constitutional in a 5-4 decision. It was unusual—although not unprecedented—for Roberts to line up with liberal justices on a divisive case.

Some otherwise thoughtful journalists leapt to the conclusion that this single episode constituted a major embarrassment for prediction markets (Leonhardt 2012) and considered it to be payback time for those highfalutin economists who have been pontificating on the superiority of their methodology. But it wasn't payback time. It was a "teachable moment" for exploring the complexities of assessing good judgment in messy real-world settings. The journalists focused on the wrong level of analysis—the individual case, instead of the population of all cases for which the market had generated predictions. Prediction-market proponents correctly noted that a 75-percent probability of x implied a 25-percent probability of not-x, so we should expect not-x 25 percent of the time. It is as if one drew lots—and happened to pick the 25-percent-probability lot. Something rather unlikely occurred. In this view, far from falsifying prediction markets, the outcome was consistent with the hypothesis that the market was perfectly calibrated.

Although the defense may look suspicious—another weaselly effort by experts caught on the wrong side of 50 percent to dodge accountability for their mistakes—the defense is 100-percent defensible. The only way to judge whether prediction markets, as a whole, tend to deliver accurate probabilities is by looking at many predictions. The only way a prediction-generating method could have been falsified by a single incident would have been if the method had assigned a probability of 1.0 to overturning the Affordable Care Act or of zero to upholding it. And prediction markets are rarely this foolish. There are almost always a few people eager to bet on long shots—and the longer the odds, the more tempted Taleb-style black-swan investors are to swoop in and take 1-in-a-billion-odds bet that should have been priced at 1 in a thousand.

Prediction-market advocates should be embarrassed if across, say, 1000 predictions in which a probability of 75 percent was assigned, the predicted outcome popped up only 50 or 60 percent of the time. This would indeed be decisive statistical evidence of overconfidence. But if across all of those predictions the predicted things happen about 75 percent of the time, the market is well calibrated. And if across all of those predictions things happen more than 75 percent of the time, the market is underconfident. In short, error is a predictable by-product of any well-calibrated forecasting system.

It would be sad to throw out an elegant method of generating realistic probabilities because of a misunderstanding of this sort. Prediction markets can integrate crowd wisdom on complex systems that no single individual can grasp. They incentivize individuals who know something that has yet to become obvious to others to make bids that move the trading prices/probabilities in the right direction—and thus also make it expensive to cling to incorrect judgments. In forecasting complex systems, we need methods that draw on diverse perspectives and update quickly—which is what liquid, well-run prediction markets do.

There is a final wrinkle. From a Jervisian perspective, a more subtle moral may lurk in this tale. As any good systems thinker knows, predictions about human affairs can influence human affairs in either self-fulfilling or self-negating directions. We will never know for sure, but Justice Roberts may have been influenced by predictions that implied he was predictable—a legacy that, perhaps, he preferred not to leave. Or he may have been swayed by the stridency of liberal reactions to the 75-percent prospect of overturning the law—and warnings that overturning Obamacare would delegitimize "his" Court. In principle, prediction markets should factor in the possible influence of their predictions of outcomes into their predictions, but there may have been a reflexivity blind spot. In this ironic twist, the critics of the markets may have been right that the 75-percent probability was wrong—but, if they were right, they were right for the wrong reason.

*   *   *

Jervis captures the elusiveness of Truth in politics. Systems thinkers recognize that there are many ways to get it wrong because there are so many layers of uncertainty in diagnosing complex systems: Which causal antecedents did we leave out—or mischaracterize? Which interconnections among which parts did we under- or over-estimate? If the net effect of reading Jervis is to induce cognitive humility about what we know about causality in real-world struggles for power, that is on balance a good thing. The benefits of a well-aimed nudge to make the overconfident a tad less so probably outweigh the risks of making the underconfident even more so.

But the benefits of systems thinking extend beyond coming to existential terms with the limits on the predictability of our world. Atul Gawande's (2009) checklist manifesto illustrates how professionals in a variety of fields—surgeons, nurses, pilots, air traffic controllers, etc.—have coped with systemic complexity more effectively by reducing it to well-rehearsed problem-solving sequences. Moreover, "more effectively" can be measured in terms of fewer secondary infections per hospital visits or fewer near-miss incidents at busy airports.

How feasible is a checklist manifesto that helps intelligence analysts and policy makers assign more realistic probabilities to possible futures across a range of political issues? The intelligence community has begun developing performance-appraisal checklists for analysts that nudge them in the direction of thinking more systematically about how they think. But it has yet—to our knowledge—taken the critical next step of checking the usefulness of the checklists against independent real-world performance criteria, such as the accuracy of current assessments and future projections.

Our experience in the IARPA forecasting tournament makes us cautiously optimistic that this next step is both feasible and desirable. Before accepting the limits on predictability, systems thinkers should push those limits, and, given the stakes and asymmetric costs of errors, we think pushing really hard is a good idea.

REFERENCES

Armstrong, J. Scott. 2006. "Findings from Evidence-Based Forecasting: Methods for Reducing Forecasting Error." *International Journal of Forecasting* 22(3): 583–98.

Gawande, Atul. 2009. *The Checklist Manifesto: How to Get Things Right*. New York: Metropolitan Books of Henry Holt and Company.

Hardin, Garrett. 1963. "A Second Sermon on the Mount." *Perspectives in Biology and Medicine* 6: 366–71.

Jervis, Robert. 1976. *Perception and Misperception in International Politics*. Princeton: Princeton University Press.

Jervis, Robert. 1997. *System Effects: Complexity in Political and Social Life*. Princeton: Princeton University Press.

Jervis, Robert. 2010. *Why Intelligence Fails: Lessons from the Iranian Revolution and the Iraq War*. Ithaca, N.Y.: Cornell University Press.

Kahneman, Daniel. 2011. *Thinking, Fast and Slow*. New York: Farrar, Straus and Giroux.

Keil, Frank C. 2010. "When and Why Do Hedgehogs Differ?" *Critical Review* 22(4): 415–26.

Leonhardt, David. 2012. "When the Crowd Isn't Wise." *The New York Times*, 8 July. http://www.nytimes.com/2012/07/08/sunday-review/when-the-crowd-isnt-wise.html?_r = 1

Mauboussin, Michael. 2012. *The Success Equation: Untangling Skill and Luck in Business, Sports, and Investing*. Boston: Harvard Business Review Press.

Mearsheimer, John J., and Stephen Walt. 2007. *The Israel Lobby and U.S. Foreign Policy*. New York: Farrar, Straus, and Giroux.

Nagel, Rosemarie. 1995. "Unraveling in Guessing Games: An Experimental Study." *The American Economic Review* 84(5): 1313–26.

Suppe, Frederick, ed. 1977. *The Structure of Scientific Theories*. Champaign: University of Illinois Press.

Surowiecki, James. 2005. *The Wisdom of Crowds: Why the Many Are Smarter than the Few and How Collective Wisdom Shapes Business, Economies, Societies and Nations*. New York: Doubleday.

Tetlock, Philip. 2005. *Expert Political Judgment: How Good Is It? How Can We Know?* Princeton: Princeton University Press.

Tetlock, Philip, and Aaron Belkin, eds. 1996. *Counterfactual Thought Experiments in World Politics: Logical, Methodological, and Psychological Perspectives.* Princeton: Princeton University Press.

Tetlock, Philip, and Barbara Mellers. 2011. "Intelligent Management of Intelligence Agencies: Beyond Accountability Ping Pong." *The American Psychologist* 66(6): 542–54.

Waltz, Kenneth N. 2012. "Why Iran Should Get the Bomb: Nuclear Balancing Would Mean Stability." *Foreign Affairs* 91(4): 2–5.

Robert Jervis

CONCLUSION: *SYSTEM EFFECTS* REVISITED

ABSTRACT: *System effects often stand in the way of attempts to come up with simple explanations of politics. Systems are often characterized by nonlinearities, where an effect is more than the sum of the effects of the actions taken by multiple actors. Another system effect is feedback, where the effect of actions is to amplify the problem the actions are intended to solve. There may also be indirect effects, where an incidental aspect of an action becomes more important (to other actors) than the primary intention; contingencies, such that an effect is not inevitable but depends on idiosyncratic or even anti-strategic initial actions; interaction effects, where the behavior of an actor changes the environment of action, so that other actors do not respond as anticipated; and unintended consequences, where the long-term or secondary effects of an action differ from the intended effect. Each of these system effects can frustrate scholarly attempts to understand political behavior using simple models of action, and, even more, can frustrate the attempts of political decision makers to predict the effects of their actions.*

At the risk of discouraging sales of my other books, I must confess that *System Effects: Complexity in Political and Social Life* (Princeton University Press, 1997) is my favorite. It is not so much that I enjoyed writing it more than I did the others (although it was a particular pleasure to be able to read almost anything and claim it was research) as that I think its ideas and approach make a greater contribution to understanding our political and social world. Yet it has had less influence on the study of political science and international politics than most of my other work.[1]

Robert Jervis, Department of Political Science and School of International Affairs, Columbia University, is the author, most recently, of *Why Intelligence Fails* (Cornell, 2010).

System Effects is highly relevant to public policy, but it rarely comes up in my discussions with officials in Washington, unlike my work on signaling, perception, the security dilemma, and nuclear deterrence. The main exceptions are two conferences sponsored by the armed forces. Perhaps contrary to popular belief, military officers tend to be intellectually sophisticated; the range of problems they have to deal with, the diversity of fields of knowledge on which they draw, their stress on the importance of what they call "situational awareness," and their knowledge that they operate in complex environments, make them more open to new ideas—both good and bad—than their civilian counterparts in the foreign-policy apparatus.

Between Disciplines

Thus, I am particularly gratified that distinguished scholars in different fields have accepted the invitation to write about the phenomena I discussed, just as I have been pleased by the fact that colleagues in economics, sociology, and biology have found *System Effects* relevant to their work and that it has found its way into the curriculum of at least one medical school.

There may be a connection between this wider interest in the book and, in contrast, the paucity of political-science research building on it—stemming, on the one hand, from the nature of academic disciplines and, on the other, from the fact that system effects are both pervasive and elusive.

However, I do not fault my political-science colleagues for failing to explicitly use *System Effects*. I have not written major follow-up studies, as Richard Posner (2012) points out, partly because world politics after September 11, 2001 has taken much of my attention, and partly because I have not found the next steps along the path from *System Effects* to be clear. As Andrea Jones-Rooy and Scott Page (2012) note, new tools, especially mathematical ones, have been developed to elucidate some of these phenomena, but they are not fully compatible with my research style. The failing is not mine alone, however, which indicates that something broader is at work.

Although political science has seen some network analysis and agent-based modeling, the highly mathematical work that is now so important in the discipline has not led many scholars into these areas. Part of the reason, pointed out by Nuno Monteiro (2012), is that in recent years political science has moved away from theories and has stressed the testing of propositions, often quite narrow ones. Relatedly, while its concern with causation is not incompatible with my book's focus on mechanisms, the discipline's desire to pin down causation by eliminating selection effects, reciprocal causation, and endogeneity, while admirably heightening rigor of expression and testing, leads to a downplaying of the importance of these phenomena not—or not only—as threats to causal inference but as fundamental forces operating in the world. Indeed, as Monteiro notes, the book questions the utility of causation in many contexts. He is too kind to point out, however, that I was—and remain—less than consistent about how much traditional notions of causation can be maintained.

The study of system effects hasn't been integrated into political science and policy research for other reasons: It does not fit the standard categories of political science; it requires interdisciplinary research; and the whole enterprise is one of high risk. Thus, several private and public foundations declined the opportunity to support this work, partly because it was not clear where it would lead. These problems mean that I cannot in good conscience urge students to adopt this approach for their dissertations, and this generates a malign form of positive feedback, since much of the best and freshest research comes at the dissertation stage.

The fact that system effects such as nonlinearities, feedbacks, indirect effects, contingencies, interaction effects, and unintended consequences are not unique to the political realm is another reason why they are not at the center of the discipline's research agenda. On the flip side, the interdisciplinarity of *System Effects* makes it useful to people outside my own field. Indeed, while some of the chapters discuss problems and the literature in political science, the basic framework and concluding chapters (which I view as the most important ones) could not have been written without knowledge of ecology, evolutionary theory, psychology, and game theory (especially the way it was done by Thomas Schelling [1960 and 1978])—but they could have been written without knowledge of political science.

The pervasive but non-obvious nature of system effects also explains why they are worth thinking about. Let me give just three examples. The ideas of interconnections and indirect effects illuminate how the introduction of cell phones in India contributed to the spread of AIDS:

They allowed prostitutes to make their own arrangements with clients, thereby enabling them to move out of brothels. Brothels, however, had been good sites for enforcing the use of condoms (Harris 2012). The Arab-Israeli conflict provides two other examples, the first of which shows both that some actors can try to make use of indirect effects and that others' behavior may depend on their not being aware of this. One reason that Israel and the United States were taken by surprise when Egypt launched the 1973 October War was that, realizing that the Arab countries could not re-take the territories lost in 1967, they thought the danger of war was quite low. They did not understand, however, that Egypt's Sadat was counting on using a military conflict, not for conquest, but to show the world that the status quo was not stable and that other powers needed to become involved. The final example shows that game-theory thinking can bring to the surface the fact that actors usually try to anticipate how others will behave, knowing that the others are doing likewise (although of course they may not do so accurately, as Israel did not in 1973). In November 2012, Israel's Iron Dome missile-defense system performed admirably in protecting against rockets fired from Gaza, but by doing so may have allowed the Palestinians to attack with relative safety. That is, without these defenses, Israel almost surely would have responded to the attacks with a ground invasion, something Hamas very much wanted to avoid, and so it might not have launched anything like the barrage that it did had Israel remained undefended.

Between Micro and Macro

A strength and a weakness of *System Effects* is that it is in-between on a number of dimensions. Most obviously, it explicates how action is situated within an interconnected and interactive system. But although I was influenced by systems theories in International Relations, including the most influential book in the field, Kenneth Waltz's *Theory of International Politics* (1979), I was not seeking to be as abstract and parsimonious as that book was. In fact, my book could be seen as anti-theoretical, not in the sense of abandoning abstractions, but rather in questioning the utility of a unified overarching theory. But I also was not engaged in either proposition testing or in developing detailed case studies. Rather, the point was to elaborate and draw attention to a wide variety of processes and mechanisms that characterize systems across diverse realms.

Similarly, the processes I examined fall between the macro and the micro, and are often connected. I tried to maintain strong micro foundations, avoid teleology and functionalism, and, like the collection of Schelling's essays (1978) that so strongly influenced me, sought to see how micro motives lead to macro behavior. They rarely do so through simple additivity or aggregation, but it is nevertheless vital to trace the links that are involved at the individual level. Often, of course, the result is not something the individual actors favored or foresaw. For example, many of the diagnoses of the 2008 financial crisis pointed a finger at cognitive pathologies on the part of the main players, whose behavior not only brought harm to the entire economy, but ended up destroying many of their own careers and at least some of their fortunes. But the pathology was collective, not individual, and the much-ridiculed saying of one of the leading participants got it exactly right: "As long as the music is playing, you've got to get up and dance."[2] That is, each financial institution had strong incentives to engage in risky behavior, not only to produce high yields for the individuals and institutions, but because if they did not do so they would have lost their customers. Some people may have been irrational, but overall it was the collective outcome rather than the individual calculations that was so.

The Problem of Prediction

This example also brings up a third way in which system effects fall in-between. As Philip E. Tetlock, Michael C. Horowitz, and Richard Herrmann (2012) note, my approach has an ambiguous stance toward prediction. On the one hand, the fact that the links between individual actions and resultant outcomes can often be traced means that an omniscient observer should have been able to find them, or at least estimate their probabilities, ahead of time. On the other hand, we don't have access to omniscient observers. Many people realized that there was a housing bubble, but it was hard to discern the more detailed interconnections among the investment instruments, how they ended up pervading an entire financial system, and the ways in which the failure of one institution would bring down others. Psychological biases may have played a role, as those involved did not want to face the tradeoff between short-run profits and the health of their institutions (and their own careers) over the long run, but it was hard to know that this was a disaster waiting to happen, let alone to predict the exact timing of it—especially because it depended in part on what everyone else believed.

Prediction is often—but not always—easier when elements are not so interconnected. Even when they are, I agree with Jones-Rooy and Page and with Tetlock, Horowitz, and Herrmann that a sensitivity to the importance and prevalence of system effects does help us predict, except, of course, that there are often many such effects at work. To put this another way, thinking of system effects reminds analysts and policy-makers that there always will be knock-on effects, indirect results, and second-order consequences. Sometimes observers and participants can anticipate them (although what happens can be affected by whether other actors anticipate them). Even when they cannot do so with any specificity, understanding the kind of ramifications that are likely will aid them in diagnosing the situation and prepare them politically and psychologically to deal with it. Those who think that action, even—or especially—strong and decisive action, will put an end to things are not only almost always wrong, but will be unable to understand what is happening and respond appropriately.

Now let me turn to some more specific system effects.

Evolution and Chronology

We are all familiar with the basic principles of evolution of change through natural selection. Of course there is much more to it than that. Darwin himself also stressed sexual selection (where the choices of one or both partners can depend on the characteristics of a desirable mate, which can be different from characteristics that have the greatest survival value), and recent research has reinvigorated arguments about whether selection operates at the level of the gene, the individual, or the group.

Fascinating as these arguments are, more relevant here is that the common idea of actors (and their offspring) changing to adapt to a static environment is misleading. In both the natural and social world, actors shape the environment just as they are shaped by it, often in ways they do not appreciate. This is obvious in the study of ecology, where the growth or decline of any one kind of plant or animal affects many others, and indeed can alter the soil, topography, and even the local climate. I cannot resist re-using a quote from *System Effects*: In describing the East African plains, a Maasai explained that "cows grow trees, elephants grow grasslands" (Western 1993, 54; also see Bescheta 2003). By eating grass, cows clear the land so that trees can sprout; elephants eat leaves and destroy trees, opening the way for grasses to thrive.

Multiple actors and environments often are involved, but we can also see co-evolution at work between two actors. Each is, in effect, the other's environment, and over time each changes it in a way that alters, if not its own behavior, then at least the results of its behavior. Although this can be apparent in retrospect when we trace the reactions of both parties to something that happened long before, the connections and processes often are obscure and indeed will appear only if one is looking for them.

A nice if disputable example is provided by Sergei Khrushchev's account of his father's behavior in the early 1960s. The Americans thought of the loss of one of their U-2 spy planes over the Soviet Union in 1960 as an unfortunate incident that, in the grander scheme of things, mattered relatively little. And when American observers and policy makers came to interpret Khrushchev's behavior in the subsequent years, they rarely mentioned this episode. They were wrong, according to Sergei, who argues that Khrushchev's outrage at the spying "would be reflected in the harshness of Father's position in the Vienna summit in 1961 and would also largely determine Soviet conduct during the deployment of Soviet missiles in Cuba [when he routinely used deception]. Father's wounds never healed. The deception on the part of his 'friend' General Eisenhower, who had gone on walks with him at Camp David and agreed that nothing was more terrible then war, struck Father to the heart" (Khrushchev 2000, 390). Of course this account is suspect in being exculpatory, and Khrushchev had used deception, bluff, and belligerent bargaining tactics before. But I do not think that we can entirely discount the possibly that the continuation of the U-2 flights after Camp David altered Khrushchev's outlook and behavior. Despite Eisenhower's reservations about authorizing these flights because he feared the consequences for American-Soviet relations, after the incident happened, neither he nor, even more, the members of the Kennedy administration understood that Khrushchev's perceived environment had changed and that he might act differently.

More generally, Lawrence Freedman (2004; also see Lieberman 2012) correctly notes that longitudinal studies of deterrence are extremely useful, but remain underdeveloped. In some cases failure at one point stems from early deterrent successes that increased the adversary's grievances. In others a subtle hint of retaliation may suffice because previous incidents have led the challenger to expect the state to stand firm. More broadly, such interactions can be seen as variants of the spiral model and the security dilemma, in which conflict is heightened by each side's attempt to increase its security, with the result that both become less secure (Jervis 1976; Booth and Wheeler 2008; Tang 2010). Each side's actions alter the environment in which the other operates, in this case to malign ends. At a certain point, furthermore, the changes induced in each side by both the other side and the interaction itself may penetrate so deeply into its perceptions, preferences, values, and domestic institutions that the hostility may become irreversible. Changes in the environment can produce fundamental changes in the agents.

The mutual molding at work is easy to overlook, especially when we focus on one actor alone. Thus it is often argued that President Nixon could have gained the same dismal settlement eventually reached in Vietnam four years earlier, saving 15-20,000 American lives and probably ten times as many Vietnamese. But one does not have to approve of Nixon's policy to see that this analysis is too simple in several ways. With the extra time, the North Vietnamese dropped the demand that the U.S. overthrow the Thiêu-Kỳ regime. And had it not been for Watergate, the threat of renewed bombing might have been sufficient to deter the North Vietnamese invasion that sealed the fate of the South in the spring of 1975. More importantly for systems arguments, the environment in 1973, when the agreement was signed, was very different from that which Nixon confronted when he was inaugurated in 1969, during a period of high tension. Four years later, a Soviet-American détente had been achieved and Sino-American relations had undergone a sea change. The landscape in which Nixon operated had thus drastically altered, and the defeat in Vietnam had much less impact than it would have had earlier. Furthermore, it is at least arguable that Nixon's continuation of the Vietnam struggle contributed both to détente and to the opening to China. Although this is far from certain, the very tensions created by the war—including the sharp escalation in the spring of 1972, when Nixon mined North Vietnamese harbors—gave the Soviets incentives to seek common ground elsewhere. For Nixon's part, the war gave him additional reasons to show that he was not a warmonger. And the tensions between the Soviet Union and China made the latter more willing to reach understandings with the United States, while defenders of the president's policy would argue that his continuing support for his South Vietnamese ally gave Chinese leaders reassurance that he would stand by them as well. Thus, it is quite possible that the new environment that Nixon faced in 1973 was created at least in part by his policies. This was not the way he expected things to work out, as the interactions were complicated and he was strongly driven by his pre-existing (and incorrect) views of how the war in Vietnam and relations with the Soviet Union might interrelate. But the effect was nevertheless important.

Much of Nixon's policy toward the USSR similarly reveals each side changing the other in ways that were consequential and unforeseen. At the start, Nixon and Kissinger believed that they could end the Vietnam War through linkage—i.e., they told the Soviet Union that they would enter arms-control negotiations only after the Soviets put pressure on North Vietnam. This was a dismal failure, because the assumptions that the Soviets had this kind of leverage and that they cared much more about arms control than did the Americans were incorrect. What happened instead was that step by step, without fully realizing it, the American leaders were drawn into trying to end the war in other ways and to entering arms-control negotiations which, although not reaching the original American goal of warding off the vulnerability of American land-based missiles, helped produce much better relations with the USSR. This change increased Chinese incentives to establish ties with the United States and also created a world in which China and the USSR saw that their interests would be better served by peace rather than war in Vietnam. So in the end there *was* a form of linkage, but one very different than Nixon and Kissinger had believed would operate.

The path to the important agreements over Berlin and Germany was similar in that the steps taken by each player (crucially including both East and West Germany, although I put them aside here) changed the other's perceptions and incentives, which in turn meant that each state faced a different environment, with the whole process representing co-evolution. We know less about the Soviet side of the story, but it is clear that when Nixon and Kissinger came into office they saw Berlin not as an opportunity to remove a fundamental source of friction, but as an annoying if minor problem brought about by assertive West German actions and a dangerous response by East Germany and the USSR (Department of State 2007). Any new agreement, they believed, would rest on the credibility of American threats and so could not provide any greater security than the status quo. In fact, thanks in part to the skill of West German leaders, the East Germans and Soviets became open to significant guarantees and the American probes produced a willingness to compromise that, much to the surprise of Nixon and Kissinger, led them into quite a different place than they were in before. Indeed, their lack of full comprehension of what was happening may have smoothed the way because, far from proclaiming the agreements as the enormous American victory that they proved to be, they played down their importance, which facilitated Soviet and East German willingness not only to sign, but subsequently to deepen relations with the West in a way that helped undermine the Soviet empire. As an added bonus, the United States stumbled on another form of linkage: the Soviet interest in having West Germany ratify the relevant treaties contributed to its willingness to go ahead with the summit in the spring of 1972, despite the American bombing of North Vietnam and the mining of its harbors.

Causation is not absent here, but is complex as it works through multiple links, ones that were not foreseen by the participants and that can be hard to trace in retrospect (such that even if I were to expand my previous analysis with much greater historical detail, it would still be easy to dispute). Each actor is changing in varying ways and degrees as it responds to the other, and with enough elements in motion, seeking the separate importance of each may be not only difficult, but misguided. As Monteiro (2012) notes, I strongly endorse Garrett Hardin's (1963, 73) statement that "in a system you cannot do just one thing," as actions both ramify and play out through the interaction with what others do, either simultaneously or in response.

This also raises difficulties for the comparative method at the heart of much standard social science. We seek causation by comparing situations that are the same on all dimensions except for one to see if the latter makes a difference. Thus, IR scholars often look at multiple confrontations between two countries or alliances and ask why the outcome varies. Why, for example, were a series of crises in the early twentieth century resolved peacefully while that of July 1914 led to war? Why did the Soviet Union maintain its overall policy in the face of containment for 40 years and then switch to conciliation and concessions—indeed unilateral ones? The obvious line of inquiry is to look at what was different in the later interactions. Whether we do this through case studies or statistical analysis, we usually treat the instances of interaction that we are comparing as though they were independent of each other. But, as indicated by the previous analysis (and many other historical accounts), more than one thing may have changed, as earlier incidents altered actors' perceptions and calculations, and sometimes their basic preferences and values.

Causation is difficult to establish by comparisons that treat the cases as separate. When a policy fails several times and then succeeds (or succeeds in a series of cases and then fails), observers are prone to attribute causation to whatever differences in the policies they can find. But it may also be that the earlier applications of a policy had changed either the situation or the other actors (or both) in a way that led to a different outcome. Thus, while defenders of President Reagan argue that the fall of the Soviet Union was largely attributable to his more vigorous and confrontational policy, others claim—correctly, I believe, although proof one way or the other is beyond us—that the differences in American policy over time mattered much less than the steady pressure that, much as George Kennan had foreseen at the start, accelerated the decay within the USSR and undermined confidence in the system at all levels of society. At the other end of the political spectrum, the argument that the Cold War ended because of "New Thinking" on the Soviet side does not appreciate the extent to which these intellectual trends were the product of the failure of the Soviet system to produce favorable results internally or externally, which, in turn, is partly explained by Western containment policy. The comparative method would focus on what seems to be new in the late 1980s, but this would neglect the changes that had been produced by the policies and interactions over the previous years.

Perhaps more often, the repetition of a successful policy can lead to failure. Too many antibiotics lead through natural selection to the spread of resistant strains. When one side coerces the other into backing down in a series of confrontations, the growth of the other's incentives to stand firm the next time may cause the policy to work out very differently than it did before.

Indirect Effects and Unintended Consequences

To say that in a system we cannot do just one thing implies, *inter alia*, that any action will have second-order or knock-on effects. We often think of these as subsidiary in the sense that they are smaller or less important than the initial effect, and we also often assume that it is the latter that is what the actor intends. But neither of these statements is necessarily correct. As actions ramify through a system, the effects can grow more rather than less powerful. The introduction or removal of a species always produces multiple knock-on effects, few of which could have been predicted ahead of time. In medicine, the "side effects" are often tolerable and smaller than the main therapeutic ones, or else the medicine would not be prescribed. But the body acts in complex ways, and in a small but not insignificant number of cases the side effects become dominant. Occasionally, of course, they can be benign, but more often they cause harm, with severe consequences and even death being possible.

We (both observers and actors) often lose sight of indirect effects because they are, well, indirect, and therefore harder to see. Yet they can be more important than the direct ones. Thus in the 2012 presidential election, as in almost all others, the vice-presidential candidates did not matter—or rather, they did not matter directly. But by nominating Paul Ryan, Mitt Romney recast the contest as a choice between two quite different economic worldviews rather than as a referendum on Obama's performance in office, and this may have been very consequential. More complexly, the collapse of a pyramid scheme in Albania in 1977 led to rioting and the looting of government buildings, including arsenals. Many of these weapons found their way across the border into Kosovo, fueling the growth of the Kosovo Liberation Army, whose increased activities precipitated a Serbian crackdown, the resulting NATO war, the expulsion of Kosovars, and the eventual independence of the country.

At least some of the discussion of positive feedback, tipping points, and path dependence can be seen as representing the power of second-order effects (Schelling 1978, chs. 4–5; Page 2006; Jones-Rooy and Page 2012). Actors sometimes try for "bank shots" in which the desired outcome occurs only after several intermediate steps. But unlike pool or billiards, in social systems human calculations, perceptions, and expectations are involved.

In relatively simple cases, people follow the Chinese adage, "kill the chicken to impress the monkey": they act against a fairly weak adversary to show stronger adversaries that, if needed, they will act against them too. Kissinger (1979, ch. 21) was very explicit that the American "tilt" against India in the crisis that led to East Pakistan becoming Bangladesh in 1971 was motivated not by the justice of the case or even the direct American interests, which were minimal, but by the felt need to show China, with which the United States was trying to build a relationship (implicitly aimed at the Soviet Union), that America would not abandon its allies or allow countries supported by the USSR to prevail. Most scholars ridicule this behavior as immoral pseudo-realism that had no basis in how countries actually behaved, but a definitive judgment must await the openings of the Chinese archives, since at this point we have little evidence about how China interpreted the American behavior, let alone how it might have viewed a different American policy.

Even more infamously, one of the standard (if debatable) explanations for why the United States fought in Vietnam was that a succession of presidents believed that not to do so would lead both allies and adversaries to conclude that the United States would not stand by its other interests and commitments. Schelling (1960) argues that a state can prevail in a dispute by committing itself to prevailing. The heart of his case is the "interdependence of commitments"—i.e., the belief that going back on one's word in one instance will undercut the credibility of one's other promises. Although the large and important topic of the perceived and actual role of reputation is beyond my scope here, it clearly is implicated in indirect effects.[3]

Much may depend on whether others believe that the state is seeking indirect effects. If the monkey thinks that you have killed the chicken to impress it, will it be as impressed? Does the message carried by the act depend at least in part on others believing that it was carried out for its own sake and that no message was intended? If observers believe that a state believes that a reputation for characteristics like honesty or toughness is very valuable, then shouldn't it discount the behavior that seems to display such attributes?

To return to the example of Vietnam, costly as the fighting was to the United States, it was vastly cheaper than having to fight for Western Europe or allowing the Continent to be dominated by the USSR. So a United States that was resolved enough to suffer significant costs, but not resolved enough to engage in a fight that would run high risks of escalating to nuclear war, could rationally choose to wage war in Vietnam. However, a Soviet Union that understood this reasoning would be less impressed with the implications of the Vietnam commitment, which in turn would mean that sticking to that commitment would not have had the desired indirect effect.

This is a crucial way in which systems composed of humans differ from those in the physical world or even those composed of animals. System effects are common in the former case, as the "butterfly effect" on climate and studies of ecology shows. And when animals either clash or cooperate, they either must judge what others are likely to do or must be hard-wired by evolution to behave as though this is what they are doing. Humans carry this a step further, however, in knowing that others are trying to guess how they are guessing what the others will do. (In principle, infinite regresses are possible, but most people stop the process after a few steps.) Expectations of indirect effects can have varied and multiple consequences. In some cases, actors will refrain from taking an action whose immediate effect is desired, on the ground that what will eventually occur is not good. Self-control leads us to (try to) limit our indulgences because we know what will follow. In a slightly less straightforward way, a person's belief that a substance is addictive or that he is particularly susceptible to addiction will inhibit initially pleasurable encounters. This process is more dynamic than the previous one because taking the substance or engaging in the behavior changes the person in a way that makes further use and abuse harder to resist.

An interesting international case illustrates the role of changing knowledge and of a greater number of steps. According to the "spillover" theory, European regional integration developed as small moves in that direction, intended for only limited objectives, induced pressures for more far-reaching integration as various groups in the participating states turned their lobbying attention to the supra-national authorities in the belief that further diminutions of national sovereignty were needed to further their interests (Haas 1958). This effect was unknown and unintended by most of the actors, and it was the great virtue of the research to have uncovered it. The effect of this knowledge was also interesting, however. I am told that when researchers asked leaders in Central America why they had not undertaken limited measures to integrate their economies, they replied that thanks to the research on Europe, they knew where such efforts would take them, and because they did not want to go that far they would not take any steps at all. (The irony here is that the researchers who studied European integration approved of it and hoped that it would be replicated elsewhere.) In other cases, actors may have to act despite being unable to stop foreseen but undesired indirect effects. When pondering whether the United States had to enter World War I, Woodrow Wilson worried that if it did, it would mean the end of the domestic reforms that he had favored. This not only turned out to be the case, but Wilson himself came to espouse suppression of dissent, contradicting his previous principles.

The question of whether actors expect indirect effects is important to the debate about institutions between institutionalists and realists in international relations. Institutionalists emphasize that institutions can facilitate cooperation. Realists, at least defensive realists, have no trouble with this emphasis (Jervis 1999). For them, institutions are one of many tools of statecraft, including cooperation, that can be used to further state interests. What gives realists trouble is institutionalists' central claim: that establishing an institution sets in motion processes that eventually alter actors' incentives, expectations, and even values in a way they did not seek or foresee, giving the institution much greater autonomy than it had at the start. This is what is meant by the argument that "institutions have a life of their own," affecting actors in unexpected ways, as was the case with regional integration.

Similarly, analysts who focus only on the obvious, immediate aims of actors' behavior will often be misled. From the mid-1950s to the mid-1970s a great many diverse actions were designed to prevent West Germany from acquiring nuclear weapons, although this was not the immediate or obvious point of the behavior. For example, one (but only one) of Khrushchev's reasons for triggering the Berlin Crisis in 1958 was to force Germany's allies to maintain its non-nuclear status. And one of the reasons that Great Britain pressured India not to develop nuclear weapons in the mid-1960s was that if it did, it would make "the prospect for the successful conclusion of a non-proliferation agreement preventing West Germany from acquiring nuclear weapons . . . almost impossible" (Schrafstetter 2001, 94). A similar motive played a contributing role in LBJ's Vietnam policies, as he thought that defeat in Southeast Asia might lead India and Japan to pursue nuclear weapons, which would increase the likelihood that West Germany would do so (Gavin 2004, 123).

More generally, changes in relations between two actors can have great impact on the system by changing the power of third parties. For both the United States and China, gaining leverage over the USSR was one of the main motives for their rapprochement, and was possibly the main motive. The other side of this coin is that increased frictions between two countries open a space for others to exert greater influence.

Sometimes third parties egg the other two on in order to achieve this result (Crawford 2011), but it often occurs inadvertently, as when Germany was the main beneficiary of the rift between France and Britain created by the latter's occupation of Egypt in 1882. Here, events made Bismarck's skills unnecessary, but they were crucial in managing the complex arrangements within Europe. In this endeavor he was a master of using indirect effects, as when he pointed out to British leaders in 1887 that if they patched up their differences with Russia, this would menace Austria-Hungary and compel it to "seek an understanding with Russia at any price. The result would be a new Three Emperors League," which would not be in the British interest (Rich 1965, 213). By marshaling others' threats to Russia and holding out to it the possibility of limited gains, he was able to maintain decent relations with it while simultaneously supporting its adversary, Austria-Hungary, and to bring a form of stability to the restless system. By contrast, Bismarck's successors believed both that Russia would always be hostile to Germany and that the divisions between Germany's many potential and actual opponents were so deep that a simpler policy could bring security. They went astray because of their inability to see the second-order consequences of their moves, which among other things provided strong incentives for Russia to come to terms first with France (despite the great ideological gulf between them) and then with Great Britain (despite—or rather, partly because of—their dangerous conflicts in Asia). "By casting Russia adrift, the Germans . . . lost perhaps their most effective lever for" gaining British support (ibid., 223). The new Triple Entente among Russia, France, and Britain was also more attractive to Italy, which had previously leaned toward Germany. Another indirect effect was even more important: Germany became much more dependent on Austria-Hungary, itself now more vulnerable to the increased activities and subversion of Russia and its Serbian client.

Sometimes one actor foresees important indirect effects that are invisible to others. When Ronald Reagan announced his plans for missile defense (the Strategic Defense Initiative or SDI), he was thinking only of protecting the United States and, more idealistically, of paving the way for the abolition of nuclear weapons. But India perceived a threat from how others would respond to SDI. China would be likely to increase its nuclear forces, which would menace India even if they were not initially targeted at it; and China might then sell its older and less useful missiles to Pakistan. In addition, the increased Soviet fear of the

United States could make it less willing to support India (Tellis 2006, 118–23; also see Kennedy 2011).

It is hard even in retrospect to determine whether the world was so interconnected that indirect effects would have dominated. Obviously, it was much harder at the time. The Cold War, at least on the American side, was built on the premise of interconnection—the domino theory being the most prominent form of the underlying belief (see, e.g., Jervis and Snyder 1991). This belief displayed itself in calculations small as well as large. In July 1961, National Security Council staffer Robert Komer argued for stepping up support for the South Vietnamese government in order to "have a major anti-Communist victory . . . in the six months before the Berlin Crisis is likely to get really hot. Few things would be better calculated to show Moscow and Peiping that we mean business" (Gibbons 1986, 57). Some of the current debates about dealing with terrorism similarly center on the extent of interconnections of varying kinds. Will attacks on "militants" dissuade others or will it enrage their relatives and fellow countrymen, encouraging them to become militants themselves? Will punishing one set of terrorists or dismantling their network deter and discourage others? Each of these possible indirect effects requires opposing policies, although unfortunately both of them could operate. Of course it is also possible that neither interconnection is significant and that the direct effects are far more important. But how the United States and others will act depends in part on which (if any) of these effects is subjectively expected, and what will happen will depend in large part on how the world is objectively arranged.

More broadly, those who favor a general American foreign policy of limited engagement believe that important interconnections are implicated only in those parts of the world that are sites of important intrinsic American interests. The United States can—and should—abstain from intervention, at least with military force, in all but a few areas. Just as America did not need to fight in Vietnam in order to protect Germany, so it can permit unrest and unpleasant regimes in countries like Syria without fear of contagion or other knock-on effects that would significantly harm the United States. Others believe that globalization is not a cliché, that it is largely accurate to say that we are in one world, and that the world order cannot be neatly divided geographically or functionally. Disturbances will ramify, even if the exact pathways and timing cannot be predicted, and for the United States to fail to lead will be to sacrifice not only important values, but political and economic interests as well. Those who hold this view differ on issues like how much the United States should rely on military instruments, how (and how much) it should accommodate others, and whether international institutions are traps or valuable instruments. But they agree that perturbations cannot be easily contained.

To take just one example, here is how one analyst describes the likely consequences of the United States assenting to many of China's claims in its region (admittedly, a fairly large perturbation in itself):

> A China unchecked by a U.S. presence in the region might not engage in outright conquest, but it would be well situated to enforce claims over disputed territories and resources. Freed from having to defend against perceived threats along its maritime periphery, China could project military power further afield to advance its interests in the Indian Ocean, the Middle East, and Africa. Within China's expanding sphere of influence, U.S. firms could find their access to their markets, products, and natural resources constricted by trade arrangements dictated by Beijing. The prospects for political reform in the countries along China's periphery would also be diminished as long as the CCP [Chinese Communist Party] remained in control. And from its secure Asian base, Beijing could offer aid and comfort to authoritarian regimes in other regions. (Friedberg 2012, 51)

Interactions and Complexity

Much of *System Effects* concerns interactions and the fact that the impact of variables often is not additive. Knowing how A alone would influence C and how B alone would influence C is not enough to tell us what will happen if both A and B are present. Because Jones-Rooy and Page (2012) use China to illustrate their discussion, let me do so as well.

Most predictions about Sino-American relations take, as driving forces, factors like the strength of the Chinese economy and how democratic its politics will become. But these predictions neglect interactions and, unhelpfully, treat economic and political factors as independent of each other and of Sino-American relations.

The status of the Chinese political system and its economic growth rate affect each other, although scholars debate the ways in which this is true. But most would agree that a sharply slackening rate of growth would reduce internal stability and put great pressure on the political system, especially because the Chinese regime no longer relies on ideology for support and so must deliver the economic goods. Were this to become problematic, the regime might seek bolstering by stirring up nationalism, which could both increase the chance of international conflict and, at least in the short run, inhibit democracy. Economic growth could allow the regime to continue more or less as it is now, although if growth involved the development of independent power centers, it could undermine the current autocracy in the long run. Conversely, politics can affect growth rates, although academic theories about what kind of political system best supports a thriving economy have changed drastically over the years, and the answer may vary with changing circumstances. At one point, rational authoritarianism was seen as useful in providing stability, increasing investment, and containing demands that could throttle growth. Now democracy and the diffusion of political power are seen as more propitious. But in either case, the basic point is that we need to look at how these factors interact.

Not only do they influence each other, but the way they affect Sino-American relations is not additive. Indeed, the sign as well of the magnitude of the impact of one variable can depend on the state of the other. To take the most obvious example, the growth of the Chinese economy could have a strongly positive effect on Sino-American relations if China is becoming more democratic, but a negative effect if it remains authoritarian. Conversely, a democratic China that was struggling economically might have incentives to pursue a belligerent foreign policy, while if it were democratic and strong it would be more likely to seek a calm international environment.

Furthermore, the state of Sino-American relations influences economic and political developments in China, as well as being influenced by them, although here, too, exactly how and how much is subject to debate. It is likely, though, that extreme Sino-American tensions would make the rise of democracy less likely. Bad relations would also slow economic growth, at least if the United States limited Chinese access to its markets. Whether American policy could facilitate the growth of democracy in China is much less certain, and even more so is what specific policies would have this or the opposite effect. Some urge a vigorous American sponsorship of democracy, perhaps even linking concessions on political and economic issues to progress on this dimension, as Reagan did with Gorbachev. On the other hand, it is often argued that for the United States to associate itself with democratic movements would be to discredit them by making them appear to be pawns of the United States and "un-Chinese" if not anti-Chinese.

Implications for Retrospective Scholarship and Prospective Action

Interconnections and interactions are what make a system a system, and their operation means that looking at factors one at a time misleads us. The standard comparative method often misses the dynamics at work and ignores the ways in which earlier events and their interpretations undermine the assumption that the cases being compared are independent of each other. Interaction and the reciprocal influence of factors makes causation even more complex and problematic for scholars than it otherwise is (Jervis 2013), but scholars have the luxury of trying to sort out causation after actions have already been taken and their effects have occurred. It is much more difficult for people to predict how their actions will work their way through the system. As I noted, Bismarck was outstanding in this regard, although it is not clear how he would have needed to adjust his policies had others been as adept as he was. On the other hand, many of the successes of Henry Kissinger, who studied Bismarck, were the unintended consequences of his failure to understand how others would react.

Although I closed my book with a discussion of how understanding system effects can lead actors to take advantage of them, I would not want to claim that this is always possible. We should always ask of an action, "What will follow, and how will we and others react and change?" But we should also realize the limits to our ability to answer, or at least to do so correctly.

As Posner (2012) and Tetlock et al. (2012) note, an awareness of all these dynamics can lead to delay in the hope that additional information or analysis will clarify the situation—or may even lead to paralysis. But it also can be liberating. Perhaps the knowledge that the consequences of our actions, both personal and political, cannot be fully calculated can lead us to be more willing to do what we think is ethically correct. Being realistic about the limits of our ability to know how we can reach desired ends can make us freer to act on our ideals. When it is not possible to see around the bend, to use Jones-Rooy and Page's phrase, perhaps it is better not to try.

Posner is also certainly correct that, unlike other forms of "complexity theory," mine proposes no specific analytical method. I wish I could, but instead, less ambitiously, I am trying to develop a way of looking at the world. Although focusing on the need to trace how forces work themselves through a system, on the difficulty of doing this well, and on the unintended consequences of doing it badly may seem to undermine prospects for either full understanding or sensible action, I hope it is not too pretentious to borrow the phrase with which Darwin closed the *Origin of Species*: "There is grandeur in this view of life."

NOTES

1. John Gaddis (2002) has written a book that parallels mine about how history is to be understood, and I do not think it has had much impact on his colleagues either.
2. Charles O. Prince, former Citigroup chief, quoted in "Citi Chief on Buyouts: 'We're Still Dancing,'" 10 July 2007, http://dealbook.nytimes.com/2007/07/10/citi-chiefon-buyout-loans-were-still-dancing/
3. Both the reputation for living up to one's signals and the reputation for behaving in certain ways are involved (Jervis [1970] 1989).

REFERENCES

Bescheta, Robert. 2003. "Cottonwoods, Elk, and Wolves in the Lamar Valley of Yellowstone National Park." *Ecological Applications* 13: 1295–1309.

Booth, Ken, and Nicholas J. Wheeler. 2007. *The Security Dilemma: Fear, Cooperation and Trust in World Politics*. New York: Palgrave Macmillan.

Crawford, Timothy W. 2011. "Preventing Enemy Coalitions: How Wedge Strategies Shape Power Politics." *International Security* 35: 155–89.

Department of State. 2007. *Foreign Relations of the United States 1969–1976*. Vol. XL of *Germany and Berlin, 1969–1972*. Washington, D.C.: Government Printing Office.

Freedman, Lawrence. 2004. *Deterrence*. Malden, Mass.: Polity Press.

Friedberg, Aaron L. 2012. "Bucking Beijing." *Foreign Affairs* 91: 48–58.

Gaddis, John Lewis. 2002. *The Landscape of History: How Historians Map the Past*. New York: Oxford University Press.

Gavin, Francis J. 2004. "Blasts from the Past: Proliferation Lessons from the 1960s." *International Security* 29(3): 100–135.

Gibbons, William C. 1995. *The U.S. Government and the Vietnam War: Executive and Legislative Roles and Relationships, Part II, 1961–1964*. Princeton: Princeton University Press.

Haas, Ernst. 1958. *The Uniting of Europe*. Stanford: Stanford University Press.

Hardin, Garrett. 1963. "The Cybernetics of Competition." *Perspectives in Biology and Medicine* 7: 469–76.

Harris, Gardiner. 2012. "Cellphones Reshape Prostitution in India, and Complicate Efforts to Prevent AIDS." *New York Times*, 24 November.

Jervis, Robert. [1970] 1989. *The Logic of Images in International Relations*, 2nd ed. New York: Columbia University Press.

Jervis, Robert. 1976. *Perception and Misperception in International Politics*. Princeton: Princeton University Press.

Jervis, Robert. 1997. *System Effects: Complexity in Political and Social Life*. Princeton: Princeton University Press.

Jervis, Robert. 1999. "Realism, Neoliberalism, and Cooperation: Understanding the Debate." *International Security* 24: 42–63.

Jervis, Robert. 2013. "Causation and Responsibility in a Complex World." In *Back to Basics: State Power in a Contemporary World*, ed. Martha Finnemore and Judith Goldstein. New York: Oxford University Press.

Jervis, Robert, and Jack Snyder, eds. 1991. *Dominoes and Bandwagons: Strategic Beliefs and Great Power Competition in the Eurasian Rimland*. New York: Oxford University Press.

Jones-Rooy, Andrea, and Scott Page. 2012. "The Complexity of System Effects." *Critical Review* 24(3): 313–42.

Kennedy, Andrew B. 2011. "India's Nuclear Odyssey: Implicit Umbrellas, Diplomatic Disappointments, and the Bomb." *International Security* 36: 120–53.

Khrushchev, Sergei N. 2000. *Nikita Khrushchev: And the Creation of a Superpower*, trans. Shirley Benson. University Park: Pennsylvania State University Press.

Kissinger, Henry. 1979. *White House Years*. Boston: Little Brown.

Lieberman, Elli. 2012. *Reconceptualizing Deterrence: Nudging towards Rationality in Middle Eastern Rivalries*. New York: Routledge.

Monteiro, Nuno. 2012. "We Can Never Study Merely One Thing: Reflections on Systems Thinking and IR." *Critical Review* 24(3): 343–66.

Page, Scott. 2006. "Path Dependence." *Quarterly Journal of Political Science* 1: 87–115.

Posner, Richard. 2012. "Jervis on Complexity Theory." *Critical Review* 24(3): 367–73.

Rich, Norman. 1965. *Friedrich von Holstein: Politics and Diplomacy of the Era of Bismarck and Wilhelm II*, vol. 1. Cambridge: Cambridge University Press.

Schelling, Thomas. 1960. *The Strategy of Conflict*. Cambridge, Mass.: Harvard University Press.

Schelling, Thomas. 1978. *Micromotives and Macrobehavior*. New York: Norton.

Schrafstetter, Susanna. 2001. "Preventing the 'Smiling Buddha': British-Indian Nuclear Relations and the Commonwealth Nuclear Force 1964–68." *Journal of Strategic Studies* 24: 87–108.

Tang, Shiping. 2010. *A Theory of Security Strategy for Our Time: Defensive Realism*. New York: Palgrave Macmillan.

Tellis, Ashley J. 2006. "The Evolution of U.S.-Indian Ties: Missile Defense in an Emerging Strategic Relationship." *International Security* 30: 113–51.

Tetlock, Philip E., Michael C. Horowitz, and Richard Herrmann. 2012. "Should 'Systems Thinkers' Accept the Limits on Political Forecasting or Push the Limits? *Critical Review* 24(3): 375–91.

Waltz, Kenneth N. 1979. *Theory of International Politics*. New York: McGraw-Hill.

Western, David. 1993. "The Balance of Nature." *Wildlife Conservation* 96: 50–55.

Index

Page numbers in **bold** type refer to figures
Page numbers in *italic* type refer to tables
Page numbers followed by 'n' refer to notes

accountability ping-pong 93
action 86, 122–3
activism: political 23, 32–3, 42–3, 46–9
actors 3–4, 26, 28–9, 41, 54–6, 61–3, 108–10
Afghanistan: US government 35
Africa 37, 42, 45; East 109; resource-extraction 42
agent-based models 28–9, 41, 50n
agents 3–4, 8–12, 20n; bias interpretation 91
aggregation techniques 97
AIDS 105–6
Albania 114
American International Group Inc (AIG) 35; failure 34
analysis 77–83
Angola 42, 89
Arab Spring (2010) 23, 32–3, 46–9
Arthur, B. 29
Australia 48
Austria 11
Austria-Hungary 118
Axelrod, R. 28

balance-of-power theory 64–7
balancing 64–7
Bayesian inference software 96
Bear Stearns 35
Bednar, J.: et al. 28
behavior 1–18, 26; actor 3–4, 26, 28–9, 41, 54–6, 61–3, 108–10; agent 3–4, 8–12, 91; human 1–18, 20n; laws 4–6; micro-level 27, 49n, 106–7; state 8–12, 63, 78; universal laws 4–6
Berlin 111–12; Crisis (1958) 117, 119
between-class tip 42
Bhavnani, R. 28
bias: agents' interpretation 91
bifurcation 31
Bismarck, O.V. 5, 118, 122
butterfly effect 88–9, 116

Canada 48
causal complexity 73, 96
causal identification 57–61
causal power: identification 57–61
causation 57–61, 81, 105, 111–13, 122
cautious optimism 93
Cederman, L.E. 28
censorship 43–4, 48
Central America 116
ceteris paribus 4–5, 14–15, 19n, 61
China 5, 46–9, 50n, 90, 110–12, 114–15, 117–22; Chinese Communist Party (CCP) 120; economy 37–40; exports policy 24; Gulja (Xinjiang) 43; international system 40–2, 45–6; media censorship 43–4, 48; Open Doors Policy (1979) 39; path dependence 38–40; political activism 42–3; and US housing crisis 24, 36
chronology 108–13
Clarke, K.A.: and Primo, D.M. 29
climate change 24–5
Cold War (1947–91) 67–72, 82, 89, 109–19
commons control 71
community: intelligence 93, 99; international 78
complex network 35, **36**
complex system: IR as 78
complex-systems theory 1, 2–4, 10, 18n, 26, 27, 36, 77–83
complexity 23–50, 72–3, 120–2; analysis 81–3; theory 77–83
computer simulations 57
conflict 78–83, 109–16; Arab-Israeli 106; Bismarck/Great Britain 5; East/West Berlin 111–12; spirals 89–90, *see also* war; World War
consequences: unintended 103, 105, 113–20
constructivist process theory 57
contextual change 43–4
contextual tip 42–3
contingency 103, 105
Converse, P.E.: *The Nature of Belief Systems in Mass Publics* (1964) 1–2
Cuban Missile Crisis (1962) 12, 72

Darwin, C. 108
David, P.A. 29
De Marchi, S. 29

INDEX

decision makers 9–12, 17, 54
design-based research 60
deterrence 109–10
difficulty 77–8
direct tip 42–3, 47–8
disagreement 11–12
disciplined complexity 96
dissociationism 87
domino theory 55–6, 89–90, 119

Earle, S.A. 14, 16
East Africa 109
economic growth: China 37–40, 46–9
economic policy 15–17; China 24
economic variables 6–8
economics 77, 80; financial crisis (2008) 81, 107
economy: Central America 116
Egypt 46–8, 106, 118
election forecasting: US 6–8, 19–20n
emergence 25, 27
emergent properties 26
energy resources: Chinese consumption 37–8; oil market 46, 47
environmental factors 8–9, 108–10
error 13–14
euro(zone): forecasting 94–5
evolution 108–13
expectations 90
experimental method 58–9
explanation 87
exports policy: China 24

Facebook 32; user growth 33
failure: error 13–14
feedback 103, 105, 114; loops 89–90
financial crisis (2008) 81, 107
financial institutions: co-risk 34–5, 34
forecasting 3–4, 85–100; US elections 6–8, see also prediction
foreign policy: decision makers 9–12
formation 33–4
France 5, 78, 118; election forecasting 95
Freedman, L. 109–10
Friedman, J. 1–18
Friedman, M. 6
function 33–4

Gaddis, J. 123n
game theory 1, 3, 10, 77, 80, 82, 90–1, 94, 106
game-theory models 28–9, 57, 62–3; multiplayer 54–5
Garand, J.C. and Holbrook, T. 7
Gawande, A. 99
Germany 5, 78, 94–5, 111–12; Berlin Crisis (1958) 117, 119; Nazi expansionism 11; Occupy Wall Street 48

Gladwell, M.: *The Tipping Point: How Little Things Can Make a Big Difference* 31
Glaser, C.L. 74n
global system: energy resources 37–8, 46; oil export/import 47
Great Britain 5, 11, 78, 117–18
Guggenheim, D.: *Earth in the Balance* 31
Gulja (China) 43

Hardin, G. 91, 112
Hausmann, R.: and Hidalgo, C. 28
Hayek, F.A. 21n
Herrmann, R.: Tetlock, P.E. and Horowitz, M.C. 16, 85–100, 107–8, 122
Hetherington, M.J. 7
Hidalgo, C.: and Hausmann, R. 28
Hirshleifer, D.: Welch, I. and Bikhchandani, S. 49n
Hitler, A. 11
Holbrook, T.: and Garand, J.C. 7
Horowitz, M.C.: Herrmann, R. and Tetlock, P.E. 16, 85–100, 107–8, 122
housing market: US crisis 24, 36, 107
human behavior 1–18, 20n, *see also* actors; agents
hypothesis testing: training 91

identification: causal power 57–61; standards 58–61
in-betweenness 26
increasing returns 29–30, 39
India 5, 115, 117, 119; AIDS 105–6
Indian Ocean 120n
indirect effects 103, 105, 113–20
industry-level investment: China 39–40, 50n
inference 96
institutionalism 117
intelligence: community 93, 99; failure 10
Intelligence Advanced Research Projects Activity (IARPA): prediction tournament 94
interactions 89, 120–2; effects 2, 103, 105
interconnection 54, 122; effects 105
international community 78
international relations (IR) 1, 6, 53–74, 106, 112; complex system 78–9; systems thinking 61–4; systems typology 62; theory 71–3
international system 61; actors 55–6; China 40–2; theory 2
investment: industry-level 39–40
Iran 69, 92
Iraq 69
Israel 106

Japan 10, 12, 90, 117; decision makers 17
Jervis, R. 2–18, 20n, 29–31, 40–1, 49n, 58–69, 85, 89–93, 103–23; complexity theory 77–83; *Perceptions and Misperceptions in International Politics* (1976) 8–11, 86; *System Effects:*

INDEX

Complexity in Political and Social Life (1997) 1–2, 23, 45, 53–4, 77, 86, 103–4; *System Effects* (1997) 1, 10, 12, 14, 16, 27, 53, 56–7, 71–3
Jones-Rooy, A. 44, 48; et al. 28; and Page, S.E. 12, 23–50, 82, 104, 108, 120–2
Joyce, K.A. 28

Kahneman, D.: *Thinking: Fast and Slow* (2011) 86
Kalyvas, S. 24
Kennan, G. 11, 113
Kennedy, J.F. 72
Keynes, M. 79
Khrushchev, S. 109
Kissinger, H. 5, 111–12, 114, 122
Knight, F. 79
Komer, R. 119
Korea: North 44, 70; South 90
Kosovo War (1998–9) 114

Lamberson, P.J.: and Page, S.E. 31–2
Laver, M. 28
Lehman Brothers 35
Lewis-Beck, M.S.: and Tien, C. 19n
Libya 48, 69
litmus test 60
loose coupling 87
Lustick, I.: and Miodownik, D. 28

macro-level outcomes 27, 49n, 106–7
mathematical models 28–9, 50n
mathematics 104; tipping points 31
media censorship: China 43–4, 48
micro-level behavior 27, 49n, 106–7
Middle East 37, 46–7, 89, 92, 120; Arab Spring (2010) 23, 32–3, 46–9; political activism 46–9
military power: US 67–71
minimum wage 15, 21n
Miodownik, D.: and Lustick, I. 28
missile defense: Strategic Defense Initiative (SDI) 118
Mitchell, M. 18n
models 28–9
Monteiro, N.P. 2, 53–74, 105, 112
Morgenthau, H. 89
multipolar nuclearized state system 92

National Intelligence Estimates 93
natural selection 108
networks 33–7, 45–6; effects 25, 27
New York Times 44
New Yorker 14
Nexon, D. 67
Nigeria 38, 42
Nixon, R. 5, 110–12
non-additivity 54
non-linearities 103, 105
North Korea 44, 70

nuclear escalation 58
nuclear proliferation 58, 64–7, 67–71, 92, 117

Obama, B. 114
objective reality: and subjective belief 10
objectivism 86
Occupy Wall Street (2011) 48
October War (1973) 106
offensive realism theory 56
oil market 46; exporters/importers 47
oil spills 14, 16
Open Doors Policy (1979) 37
optimism 93–100
Ottoman Empire 5
outcomes 41, 86

Page, S.E. 30, 39, 50n; et al. 28; and Jones-Rooy, A. 12, 23–50, 82, 104, 108, 120–2; and Lamberson, P.J. 31–2
Pakistan 118
path dependence 25, 27, 29–31, 114; China 38–40
path-dependent outcomes 46
Pearl Harbor 10, 12
Pennsylvania University 85n
pessimism 88–93
phase transition 25, 31, 82
Pierson, P. 29
policy: agnosticism 92; makers 86; US 45–6, 89, 110–13
political activism: China 42–3; Middle East 23, 32–3, 46–9
political epistemology 8–13
political growth: China 46–9
political science 4–8
political theory 13–18
political tipping 43–4
Polya process 29
Portugal 11
positivism 8
Posner, R.A. 4, 16, 77–83, 104, 122–3
possibility 5–6
Potter, P.B.K. 37
power 53, 56, 59, 63, 66, 89; balancing 64–7; military 67–71; preponderant 67–71; systematic balance 64–7; US 67–71
pragmatism 86
prediction 1–18, 26, 55–6, 71, 79, 81, 89, 91–2, 107–8; accuracy 85–8; market 97–9; tournament (IARPA) 94, *see also* forecasting
Primo, D.M.: and Clarke, K.A. 29
probability 94–100
process theory 63–4
professional testing: hypothesis testing 91
psychology 18–19n

qualitativity 26

INDEX

quantitativity 26

rational ignorance theory 7–8
Reagan, R. 113, 118
realism 117
reasoning: theory-driven 93–4
reconstruction 81
relatism 87
relative power 63
research 59–60; method-driven/problem-driven 74n
resource-extraction: China/Africa 42
Roberts, J. 97–9
Romney, M. 114
Rorty, R. 72
Russia 10, 78, 118
Ryan, P. 114

Sadat, A. 5, 106
Schelling, T. 49n, 105, 107, 115
scholarship 122–3
second-order effects 114
selection 108
self-organized criticality 25
Serbia 114
Shapiro, I. 74n
simple complexity 91
Sino-American relations 110, 120–2
social science 5
social systems 55–6
South Africa 38, 42
South Korea 90
Soviet Union *see* USSR
spill-over theory 116
spiral model 110
state: behavior 8–12, 63, 78; multipolar nuclearized systems 92; relations 4–5; strategy balancing 64–7; survival 65–7
stock market 80
Strauss-Kahn, D. 95
structure 33–5; constructivism 63; realism 63; theory 61
subjective belief: objective reality 10
Syria 69
system: definition 54–5; dynamics 27
system effects 1–18, 23–50, 27–9, 103–23; China 37–8; types (Jervis) 26, 54–5
systemic theory 61
systems analysis 77–83
systems outcome: classification (Wolfram) 32
systems theory 1, 57; computer models 3

systems thinking 53–74, 85–100; IR 61–4, 71–3; IR typology 62; nuclear weapons 64–7; unipolarity 67–71

Taylor, A.J.P. 5
terrorism 119
Tetlock, P.E.: *Expert Political Judgement* (2005) 2, 94; Horowitz, M.C. and Herrmann, R. 16, 85–100, 107–8, 122; prediction strategy 18
theory-driven reasoning 93–4
Tien, C.: and Lewis-Beck, M.S. 19n
tipping points 25, 27, 31–2, 41–4, 114
Tulis, J.K.: *The Rhetorical Presidency* (1987) 2
Tunisia 32–3, 46, 48
Turkey 38

uncertainty 80
unintended consequences 103, 105, 113–20
unipolarity 53, 67–71
United Arab Emirates (UAE) 38
United States of America (USA) 5, 11, 12, 95, 106, 109–16, 114–17; Afghanistan 35; decision makers 17; election forecasting 6–8, 19–20n; elections (1992) 7; elections (2012) 114; energy resources 46; housing market 24, 36, 107; minimum-wage 15; Occupy Wall Street 48; Pearl Harbor 10; policy 45–6, 89, 110–13; preponderant power 67–71; voting behavior 6–8
universal behavioral laws 4–6
unstable equilibria 31
USSR (Union of Soviet Socialist Republics) 5, 12, 67–71, 109–18

Vietnam 89, 117, 119; War (1955–75) 110–16

Wall Street Journal: Minority Youth Unemployment Act (2013) 21n
Waltz, K. 2, 89, 92; *Theory of International Politics* 57, 106
war 58, 66–7
Weber, M. 4–6
Welch, I.: Hirshleifer, D. and Bikhchandani, S. 49n
Wilson, W. 117
within-class tip 42
Wolfram, S.: *A New Kind of Science* (2002) 27, 28; systems outcome classification 32
World War: I (1914–8) 78, 117; II (1939–45) 79, 92

www.routledge.com/9780415696234

Related titles from Routledge

Rethinking the Rhetorical Presidency

Edited by Jeffrey Friedman and Shterna Friedman

In *The Rhetorical Presidency*, Jeffrey Tulis argues that the president's relationship to the public has changed dramatically since the Constitution was enacted: while previously the president avoided any discussions of public policy so as to avoid demagoguery, the president is now expected to go directly to the public, using all the tools of rhetoric to influence public policy. This has effectively created a "second" Constitution that has been layered over, and in part contradicts, the original one. In *Rethinking the Rhetorical Presidency*, scholars of the presidency and of political theory come to grips with the new type of presidency that has created during the Progressive Era.

This book was originally published as a special issue of *Critical Review: A Journal of Politics and Society*.

Jeffrey Friedman is a visiting scholar in the Department of Government, University of Texas at Austin and editor of Critical Review.

Shterna Friedman received an MFA from the Iowa Writers' Workshop, University of Iowa. She is the managing editor of *Critical Review: A Journal of Politics and Society*

February 2012: 246 x174: 296pp
Hb: 978-0-415-69623-4
£85 / $145

For more information and to order a copy visit
www.routledge.com/9780415696234

Available from all good bookshops

www.routledge.com/9780415696180

Related titles from Routledge

The Nature of Belief Systems Reconsidered

Edited by Jeffrey Friedman

In the foundational document of modern public-opinion research, Philip E. Converse's "The Nature of Belief Systems in Mass Publics" (1964) established the U.S. public's startling political ignorance. This volume makes Converse's long out-of-print article available again and brings together a variety of scholars, including Converse himself, to reflect on Converse's findings after nearly half a century of further research.

This book was originally published as a special issue of *Critical Review: A Journal of Politics and Society*.

Jeffrey Friedman, a visiting scholar in the Department of Government, University of Texas at Austin, received a Ph.D. in Political Science from Yale University.

Shterna Friedman received an MFA from the Iowa Writers' Workshop, University of Iowa.

April 2012: 216 x 138: 416pp
Hb: 978-0-415-69618-0
£100 / $160

For more information and to order a copy visit
www.routledge.com/9780415696180

Available from all good bookshops